Swim Fast

To all those amazing Barracudas

Second Edition

Blythe Lucero

SWIM FAST

100 WORKOUTS TO IMPROVE YOUR SWIM TECHNIQUE

Meyer & Meyer Sport

British Library of Cataloguing in Publication Data
A catalogue record for this book is available from the British Library
Swim Fast
Maidenhead: Meyer & Meyer Sport (UK) Ltd., 2023

ISBN 978-1-78255-260-4

© 2009, 2023 by Meyer & Meyer Sport (UK) Ltd.
Second Edition 2023 of the First Edition 2009.
Aachen, Auckland, Beirut, Cairo, Cape Town, Dubai, Hägendorf, Indianapolis, Maidenhead, Manila, New Delhi, Singapore, Sydney, Tehran, Vienna
Member of the World Sport Publishers' Association (WSPA), www.w-s-p-a.org

Printed by Versa Press, East Peoria, IL
Printed in the United States of America
ISBN: 978-1-78255-260-4
E-Mail: info@m-m-sports.com
www.thesportspublisher.com

TABLE OF CONTENTS

INTRODUCTION

I have always been of the opinion that it is best for a swimmer to workout with a coach present. I have developed this conclusion over many years, first as a swimmer, then as a swimming teacher and coach. This opinion has been reinforced frequently, both during my own experience in the water, as an athlete in training, and then from the deck, while observing the development of swimmers.

When a coach is part of the equation, there to design training content and routines, guide the progression of development, and provide motivation and challenge when needed, a swimmer can concentrate on swimming! Of all the things a coach does, one of the primary benefits lies in his or her ability to observe stroke technique in terms of swimming efficiency. This is an important part of a swimmer's progress at all stages of development. For beginning and intermediate swimmers, the coach's observation is critical to identifying technique errors, doing it early, and giving corrective feedback long before those errors become habit. For advanced swimmers, the coach's observation takes the form of refining stroke technique, and providing reminders so the swimmer remains focused on maintaining the most efficient style even during the most strenuous training phase. I believe a coach's observation and feedback facilitates the most direct path for a swimmer's improvement.

There is an unspoken partnership between athlete and coach. In the most successful of these relationships, both are engaged in all aspects of the pursuit. A positive outcome comes from a situation where both athlete and coach are dedicated to the training program, committed to pursue improvement through specific and frequent practice, and focused on the goal. I feel that it is really too much to expect the athlete to do both jobs. Training can be extremely demanding, and as if that is not enough, life is full of distractions and responsibilities. Some days it is just easier for the swimmer to say, "I'm sleeping in today," "I'm getting out early," or "I'm going to skip that set," if not for the fact that the he or she knows that the coach is there on deck, holding up his or her end of the bargain. I believe that a strong swimmer/ coach relationship provides the strongest foundation for good results from a training program.

Having made these points, there is something to be said for self- guided discovery. If an athlete is successful in maintaining motivation, taking on challenge and remaining focused on the goal, the process of working on stroke technique can be a very valuable experience. It takes a great deal of concentration and analysis to isolate and identify stroke problems, and to refine stroke technique. A swimmer who is able to do this well, and consistently, can find the experience of working out on their own to be quite satisfactory.

Over the last 20 years, I have encountered quite a few requests for workouts that swimmers can do on their own. I have provided workouts to swimmers, on a temporary basis, to do on vacation, or on work assignment out of town. Each time I have done so, I have carefully prefaced the set of workouts with specific guidelines to the swimmer.

I will do the same here:

In addition to conditioning, the workout is your chance to practice swimming right. It is of the utmost importance to pay close attention to your stroke mechanics, and be very in tune with what makes swimming more and less efficient. Without your coach there to observe, it is now your job to identify and correct stroke problems and continually refine your technique. You must use your own senses to give you feedback. Above all, you must promise not to lose sight of the fact that every day you swim you can learn more.

This is the first in a three-book series, called "Coach Blythe's Swim Workouts." This book contains technique-based workouts, designed to help swimmers focus on the mechanics of swimming. The second book in the series contains conditioning workouts, designed to help swimmers build swimming capacity, strength and endurance. The third book in the series contains challenging workouts, designed for advanced level training. Swimmers may use the material in these books to practice and train on their own, when the swimmer's coach is not present, or to create their own training routine, with the guidelines above. Also, these books can be useful to coaches looking for workout content to use in the training programs they design for their teams.

The 100 workouts in this book focus on increasing general swimming efficiency by improving swimming technique. The workouts blend stroke drills and drill/swim bridging sets, in a format that will help build better technique, and build the endurance required to perform that technique over time. Workouts in this collection total up to 2,000 yards/meters. Specific workouts are included for each of the competitive swimming strokes. Each workout is designed as a balanced practice session unto itself, with a warm-up, progressions of technique work, progressions of effort and a cool-down.

Without the intent of discouraging anyone taking up the wonderful sport of swimming, this book is not a "learn to swim" manual. Users of the book are expected to have basic water skills, including the ability to be able to completely submerge and recover to a standing position, float, tread water, and move forward with arms and legs. As well as advanced beginner and intermediate level swimmers, this book is also appropriate for advanced swimmers seeking a "technique tune-up," in the journey toward more efficient swimming.

WORKING OUT WITH A PURPOSE

Swimmers work out to achieve better swimming. Whether you define better swimming as more swimming capacity, endurance or more speed, better swimming is more efficient swimming. The workouts in this book are designed with one purpose: to help the swimmer increase swimming efficiency by making technique improvements. A more efficient swimmer is able to expend less energy, and therefore swim longer and farther with less fatigue. Swimming can then become a more rewarding activity. A swimmer who can swim longer without getting tired can then apply his or her attention and energy to building a good base of endurance. With increased swimming capacity, the swimmer may choose to train for faster swimming.

So, this collection of workouts is part of the process of becoming a better swimmer overall. This process does not happen immediately. It takes time, focus and practice. Patience and dedication are important qualities to bring with you in this process. If attention and time are given to swimming right, endurance, capacity for yardage and speed will happen.

The basic formula to keep in mind is this:

> SWIMMING WELL + SWIMMING OFTEN = BETTER SWIMMING

SWIMMING WELL

The first element in the formula for better swimming is swimming well. Swimming is mechanically complex, and it is easy to get distracted with the effort that is initially required to get from point A to point B. Remember that it is more important to be focused on perfecting the mechanical aspects of swimming before turning your focus to swimming more and more yards.

CORRECT PRACTICE

A respected swim coach once said, "Doing a drill 99% correctly is 100% wrong." That seems harsh, but it is true. If a swimmer practices incorrectly, they are reinforcing poor technique. It is therefore a top priority to practice each drill, each stroke, each set as mechanically perfect as possible. At first it may seem very robot-like, even unnatural. Give it a chance. Remember that every skill improves with practice. Driving, typing and dancing are good examples of skills that improve with practice. We start by practicing them slowly, step-by-step. Then, gradually, they become comfortable, even automatic. There comes a time when we realize that we are performing a complex skill well, without thinking about it.

FOCUS POINTS

Each workout in this collection begins with a "Focus Point" to help swimmers zero in on specific issues that the workout emphasizes, through specially chosen drills and sets. "Focus Points" address important issues including body position, kick productivity, eliminating drag, improving feel for the water, alignment, swimming in a core-centered manner, stroke coordination and leverage. It is important to think about the particular focus point, or theme throughout the workout, in order to get the full benefit of stroke improvement exercises.

Each workout asks the swimmer to progressively build mechanical skills into a complete swimming stroke. Each step of the way, the swimmer should try to relate what he or she is asked to do to the "Focus Point." At times, it will be frustrating and confusing. Drills can be awkward and clumsy at first. Again, remember to be patient, and keep trying!

Sometimes the point of a particular drill can be elusive. If a particular drill is continually not making sense to you, ask a coach for feedback. Remember, the first step in becoming a better swimmer is to swim correctly.

As the swimmer improves each aspect of his or her stroke, it positively affects another. One by one the pieces will fall into place.

SWIMMING OFTEN

The second element in the formula for swimming well is swimming often. It is important to create a good workout routine that you can stick with. In addition to the considerations in this section, use your knowledge of your own experiences with other physical activities, and skill attainment to make a routine that works for you.

YOUR WORKOUT ROUTINE

It is well documented that frequency of practice is a key learning strategy. This means that the more often we are exposed to the skill we are trying to master, the faster the rate of learning. So, in general, a swimmer who swims four or five days a week will improve more quickly than a swimmer who swims once a week. This is something to keep in mind when planning your workout routine. If there is too much time between workouts, you will find yourself having to backtrack and repeat activities in order to refresh your memory and "feel" for the water, to regain the advances you made at your previous workout. A workout routine that keeps practice sessions closer together allows the swimmer's body and mind to hold on to the forward steps taken at the previous workout, so that valuable repetition will work to reinforce and strengthen the swimmer's understanding and muscle memory, instead of first having to re-establish it.

Workout frequency, however, must be carefully balanced with recovery time. Swimming well requires the use of almost every muscle in the body. It is a strenuous activity, especially as a swimmer is working on building capacity. Without ample rest between workouts, the swimmer cannot continue to adapt to the workload over time. A swimmer who is constantly fatigued is less motivated and less able to concentrate on the important skills they are practicing. This means that recovery time is an essential ingredient in becoming a better swimmer. So, in general a swimmer who swims four to five days a week will improve, over the long term, more quickly than a swimmer who swims seven days a week.

A workout routine of every other day is a good option for many swimmers. Some swimmers do well with a schedule of swimming two days in a row, then taking a day off. For some, swimming each weekday, then taking weekends off works well. Developing a workout routine that works for you will take some trial and error. It is also something that will change over time as your skills and capacity for swimming increases.

In general, it is important to take at least two days off a week.

Always consult a doctor before beginning a fitness routine such as this.

WHEN ENOUGH IS ENOUGH

Sometimes, there comes a point where a swimmer has reached the limit of benefit from a workout. These workouts are demanding on two levels, both physically and mentally. It is easy to fall into the trap of thinking that a workout of only about 2,000 yards is easy enough to complete. Remember, completing the workout is only part of the challenge. Benefiting from the content of the workout is more important. To make sure this is happening, regularly ask yourself the following questions during your workout:

- Am I too tired to concentrate on the point of the workout?
- Am I just doing empty yards?

If the answer to either question is "yes," then, it is time to stop. Start again tomorrow.

Also, if you find yourself struggling to make it through a set, you will not be able to concentrate on the point of the set. So, if the distances called for are overwhelming, cut them in half.

ACHIEVING BETTER SWIMMING

By swimming well, and swimming often, a swimmer arrives at better swimming. It is important to remember that achieving better swimming is a process. It doesn't happen all at once; it occurs gradually and continually. It is important to be aware of your progress, and celebrate it along the way.

MEASURING PROGRESS

Progress can be defined in many ways. Capacity for distance, and capacity for speed are two ways to evaluate progress. Ultimately, regarding this collection of workouts, progress in swimming efficiency is the most important measure of improvement.

Measuring progress requires a starting point to be established, then regular comparisons to that starting point must be done.

A swimmer's progress in terms of capacity for distance can easily be measured in yardage:

- How far can a swimmer swim, non-stop, compared to the previous week?
- How many yards can a swimmer complete in 10 minutes, compared to the previous week?

Progress in terms of capacity for speed can be measured in terms of time:

- How long does it take to swim 200 yards, compared to the previous week?
- How fast can a swimmer swim 50 yards, compared to last week?

Improvements in yardage and time can reflect improvements in swimming efficiency. An additional way to measure swimming efficiency is counting strokes:

- How many strokes does it take to cross the pool, compared to last week?
- Can the same number of strokes be maintained for four or eight lengths in a row?

As a part of your overall plan, it is a good idea to measure progress regularly, to insure that improvement is occurring and continuing. Choose a regular interval at which you measure progress, for instance once a week, or once a month. There should be enough time between measures to allow for skills to develop and progress to build, but not too much time to continue practicing in a manner that is not producing results.

If improvements are not shown, repeatedly when measuring progress, it provides important feedback. The swimmer may need:

- more time to practice each drill
- to practice the drills more precisely
- to change his or her workout routine to allow more recovery, or more exposure
- to consult a coach for observation and feedback

VALUING THE PROCESS

Improvement may not happen every single time you measure your progress. This is natural. It is not the end of the world, and it is certainly not any indication that you should give up your pursuit of better swimming. Consider that swimming in and of itself is a rewarding experience. It is good for you on all levels: physically, mentally and emotionally. Notice the muscle tone that you are gaining. Notice the things you work out in your head while you are swimming. Notice the smile on your face after you swim. Your swimming is time well spent. Enjoy every minute of it.

GETTING STARTED

This collection of workouts is organized by stroke emphasis. The first 25 workouts focus on freestyle technique. The next 25 focus on backstroke technique, then 25 on breaststroke technique, and 25 on butterfly. It is important to be familiar with the presentation of the workouts to get the most benefit from them. This section defines the terminology used within the workouts, describes the format in which the workouts appear, and finally, provides a summary of the technique drills that are called for within the workouts.

WORKOUT TERMINOLOGY

It will be important to be familiar with the following terms and swimming jargon used throughout this collection of workouts, appearing here in alphabetical order:

* **25, 50, 75, 100, 200:**
  Refers to the distance to be done in terms of a 25 yard/meter pool. A 25 would be one length, a 50 would be two lengths, a 100 would be four lengths, etc.

- **4 x 25:**
  Refers to the number of times a distance is to be done; for instance, in this example, 25 yards will be done four times.

- **50 Easy:**
  A short recovery swim, and a chance to reflect on the set that you just finished.

- **Alternating 25s (or 50s) of:**
  Calls switching between two activities after a specific distance.

- **Arms Leading:**
  The floating position with the arms extended over the head.

- **Cool-Down:**
  The final exercise period of easy, continuous swimming that is important to gradually return the heart to its regular rhythm, and rinse out the muscles.

- **Count Strokes:**
  Counting the total number of strokes it takes per length of the pool.

- **Drill:**
  An exercise designed to practice a specific skill or aspect of a stroke correctly.

- **Drill/Swim:**
  An exercise that alternates drill and swim, in order to use the skills emphasized in the drill in practice while swimming the full stroke.

- **Fast Freestyle (or other stroke):**
  Using a faster tempo, and applying more power to move across the pool faster than usual.

- **Flutter Kick:**
  The kick done with Freestyle and Backstroke, using an alternating leg action.

- **Focus Point:**
  The theme or emphasis of the workout.

- **Head Leading:**
  The floating position with the arms at the side of the body.

- **Kick:**
  Leg action only. A kickboard may be used for front flutter kick, or breaststroke kick; however, backstroke kick and dolphin kick should always be done without a kickboard. Kicking is an excellent aerobic activity and an important way to build swimming endurance.

- **Kick (other than breaststroke kick):**
  Any kick other than breaststroke kick. The reason for this is that breaststroke kick should only be done when the knees are completely warmed up to avoid injury.

- **Pull:**
  For freestyle only. Using a pull buoy to float your lower body and practice the upper-body action of the stroke, including arm stroke, roll, alignment, and use of core.

- **Stationary Drill:**
  A drill that is done without covering distance in the pool.

- **Swim:**
  An exercise using the full stroke as specified.

- **Underwater streamlined kick:**
  Kicking while totally submerged, arms extended and tight over the ears, chin tucked, core engaged to be as streamlined as possible.

- **w/15 SR:**
  Refers to the amount of rest (R) in seconds (S) between swims.
  For example, in this case: with 15 seconds' rest.

- **Warm-up:**
  Initial exercise period of sustained, medium-intensity swimming lasting at least 10 minutes, or at least 10% of your total yardage. Also an opportunity to review what you covered in your previous workout, and to refresh your "feel" for the water.

- **Your Choice:**
  Swimmer chooses the stroke or drill.

WORKOUT FORMAT

Each workout begins with a Focus Point, and ends with the total yardage. Focus Points are designed to orient the swimmer to the theme, or goal, of the workout. Total yardage is included as one measure of a fitness routine. All of the workouts in this book total about a mile, some a little more, some a little less. It is important to remember, however, that the main measure of this collection of workouts is not miles swum, but improvement in swimming technique, and increased swimming efficiency.

Workout content is presented in a sequentially, one activity after the other, using a standardized set of directions. Each activity or set appears as a string of commands. Figure 1 diagrams these commands.

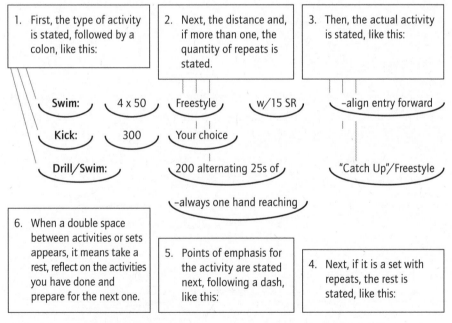

Figure 1: Explanation of workout format

SUMMARY OF DRILLS

Drills are a primary component of this collection of workouts. Drills are a way to work on a stroke, or a particular aspect of a stroke by isolating, emphasizing or repeating an exercise. The following drills are called for by name within the workouts, appearing in quotes. In this summary, they are grouped by stroke, and are listed in alphabetical order. Each drill is accompanied here by a brief description of how to perform it, and its purpose. It is important to study the drills and understand how to do them correctly to get their full benefit.

Most of these drills are also described in complete detail in my book, *100 Best Swimming Drills*. The book is an excellent resource to accompany this collection of workouts. In addition to step-by-step descriptions, each drill is illustrated, and its purpose is clearly outlined. Feedback charts also follow each drill to address common problems that can interfere with feeling the point of the drills.

FREESTYLE DRILLS

3 Kick Switch – To feel the rolling action of the stroke, kick on side for three kicks, low arm leading, other arm at your side, face in the water, then switch sides, and arm positions, and repeat (see figure 2)

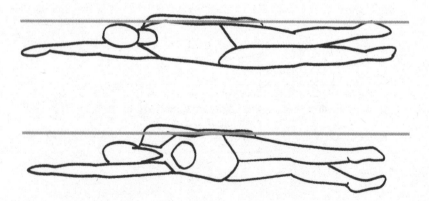

Figure 2: Kick in a side floating position, then switch sides and resume an aligned float and kick.

6 Kick Switch – To feel length of stroke and alignment, kick on side for six kicks, low arm leading, other arm at your side, face in the water, then switch sides, and arm positions, and repeat (see figure 2).

12 Kick Switch – To feel alignment, the rolling action of the stroke, and the length of the stroke, kick on side for twelve kicks, low arm leading, other arm at your side, face in the water, then switch sides, and arm positions, and repeat (see figure 2).

3 Strokes, 3 Kicks – To emphasize the rolling action of the stroke, take three regular freestyle strokes with kicking, then kick only in the side floating position, low arm leading, other arm at your side, for three extra kicks, face in the water, then do three more freestyle strokes, then kick only floating on the other side for three extra kicks, and repeat.

3 Strokes, 6 Kicks – To emphasize the rolling action of the stroke, and constant kicking, take three regular freestyle strokes with kicking, then kick only in the side floating position, low arm leading, other arm at your side, for six extra kicks, face in the water, then do three more freestyle strokes, then kick only floating on the other side for six extra kicks, and repeat.

Figure 3:

*Point forward with your thumb
in the direction you are going.*

*Avoid leading your stroke
off course with a collapsed wrist.*

All Thumbs Drill – Freestyle arm stroke extension actively pitching the wrist so the thumbs point in the direction you are swimming for better alignment and catch (see figure 3).

Catch-Up – Like regular freestyle, except one arm catches up to the other in front, emphasizing that one arm should always be reaching, and the other stroking. Start with both arms leading, then do a complete freestyle stroke with one arm, when both arms are back in the leading position, do a freestyle stroke with the other arm, continue.

Dead-Arm Freestyle – Single-arm freestyle with the still arm at your side, breathing toward the still arm side, to practice using hip rotation to breathe.

Fist Freestyle – Freestyle with fists, using the forearms to press against the water to develop a high elbow arm stroke.

Floppy Hand Drill – Regular freestyle except during each recovery, flop the hand back and forth to check for relaxation.

Freestyle With Dolphin – Regular freestyle arms with a dolphin kick each time water in front, to practice coordinating the arm and leg actions (see figure 4).

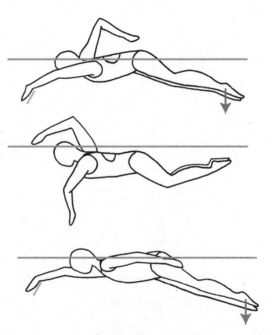

Figure 4: Freestyle with dolphin. Coordinate the downbeats of your feet with your catch.

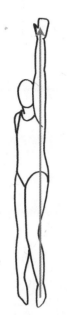

Head Lead Kick – Flutter kick with your arms at your sides to practice positive floatation.

Head-Up Freestyle – Rapid freestyle with your head up, as used in water polo, looking straight ahead to practice catching water and constant kicking.

Hip Skating – Regular freestyle with an imaginary ice skate on each hip bone in front. Achieve a skating rhythm to practice core leverage. Eventually try to feel the blade of the skate extending all the way from the hip to the fingertip of the reaching hand to feel leverage and alignment at the same time (see figure 5).

Figure 5: Skate on your hips

Log Roll – Floating in a head lead position, and kicking, do a quarter roll, hold for 5 seconds, do a quarter roll, continue, generate actions from the hips and stabilize from the core to practice core-centered swimming.

One-Arm Freestyle – Single-arm freestyle with the still arm leading to isolate the arm stroke action.

One-Leg Kick – Using a kickboard, kick rapid flutter kick with one leg only to develop a productive kick.

Pendulum – To feel core leverage, switch rhythmically, like a pendulum, from one side floating position, with low arm leading, and other arm in high elbow recovery position, to the other side, continue (see figure 6).

Figure 6: Feel the pendulum effect.

Pull/Push Freestyle – Regular freestyle isolating the pulling motion from full extension to the shoulder and the pushing motion from the shoulder to the end of the stroke past the hip (see figure 7).

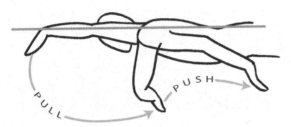

Figure 7: The path of the freestyle arm stroke underwater.

Sculling – Tracing a sideways figure-eight with the hands, press out with thumbs down, press in with thumbs up, in order to develop better "feel" for the water.

Shark Fin – To practice a well-balanced recovery, float in on your side, low arm leading, kick steadily, and raise the elbow of the high side recovering arm to a high pointing position, count to five, then return arm it to your side, continue.

Underwater Streamline Kick – Underwater kicking with arms leading in a tight, narrow body position silhouette, using a quick, compact kick to learn to eliminate drag (see figure 8).

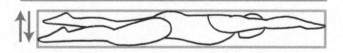

Figure 8: Compact kicking underwater in streamline.

Vertical Kicking – Stationary flutter kicking in deep water from a vertical position, vigorously enough to keep the face out of the water, to develop a productive kick.

BACKSTROKE DRILLS

Armpit Lift – Exaggerating the roll of the backstroke by lifting the armpit completely out of the water when the arm is at the highest point of recovery, to feel that the high recovering side provides leverage to the low stroking side of the body (see figure 9).

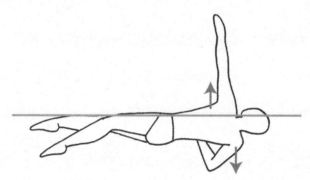

Figure 9: Lift your armpit at the high point of recovery to feel the leverage of the stroke.

Backstroke 3 Stroke Switch – To feel the rolling action of the stroke, kick on side for three kicks, low arm leading, other arm at your side, face up, then switch sides, and arm positions.

Backstroke 6 Kick Switch – To feel alignment, and the length of the stroke, kick on side for six kicks, low arm leading, other arm at your side, face up, then switch sides, and arm positions.

Backstroke 12 Kick Switch – To feel alignment, the rolling action of the stroke, and the length of the stroke, kick on side for twelve kicks, low arm leading, other arm at your side, face up, then switch sides, and arm positions.

Backstroke Balance Drill With Cup – Regular backstroke with a cup filled halfway with water balancing on your forehead to emphasize that the head should be still, while the body rolls smoothly through the stroke.

Breathing Pocket – Regular backstroke exaggerating the roll to feel a barrier from the water when the shoulder is at its highest point, and using this moment to inhale.

Boiling Water Drill – Rapid and productive backstroke kicking to practice pushing the water upward with force, so it makes a continuous boil, without the feet breaking the water's surface (see figure 10).

Figure 10: Make the water boil by snapping your foot upward, but without breaking the surface of the water.

Clock Arms – First done standing in front of a mirror, practice feeling the correct hand entry position at shoulder width or wider (at least 11:00 and 1:00). Repeat while swimming backstroke.

Corkscrew – One stroke freestyle, then one stroke backstroke, continue, feeling the deep catch of the backstroke accomplished by rolling into your stroke.

Cup on Forehead – Quarter Turn - To achieve a still or "independent head," do head leading backstroke kicking, with a cup half filled with water balancing on your forehead. Every twelve kicks, rotate your body a quarter turn, without dropping the cup. First to left, then back to flat, then to right, then back to flat, continue (see figure 11).

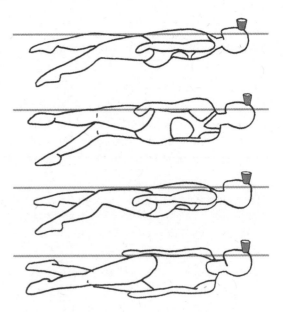

Figure 11: Achieve an "independent head."

Fist Backstroke – Backstroke with fists, using the forearms to press against the water to develop a high elbow arm stroke.

Float on Spine – Stationary drill where you practice the "banana position," a firm back floating position, where you achieve a straight spine by rolling pelvis forward and contract the abdominals, so it feels like you are in shaped sort of like a banana on your front, but very straight on your back (see figure 12).

Figure 12: Float on your spine and achieve the banana position.

Locked Elbow Recovery Drill – Backstroke, recovering with actively locked elbows for better alignment and stroke balance.

No Knees Streamline Kick – Hand leading backstroke kicking. Check for over-bent knees by holding a kickboard with one hand on the water's surface over the knees. If the knees bump the board, you are raising your knees up, rather than dropping your heel.

One-Arm Pull/Push Backstroke – Single-arm backstroke, with still arm at your side, trying to isolate the pulling motion from full extension to the shoulder, and the pushing motion from the shoulder to the end of the stroke past the hip (see figure 13).

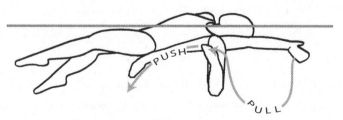

Figure 13: The path of the backstroke underwater.

One-Arm Rope Climb – Floating on your back, with a lane line or rope beside you, take hold of the line and pull your body past the point where you are holding, simulating the feeling of efficient backstroke.

Opposition Freeze Frame – Regular backstroke, stopping at various times in the stroke to feel the many balance points of the opposing arm stroke.

Pigeon-Toed Kicking – Backstroke kicking with the feet and knees turned slightly inward to a pigeon-toed position to achieve a larger foot surface to push water upward, and less drag from knees breaking the surface.

Puppy Ears – Regular backstroke, pitching the hands actively outward from the wrist during recovery, like a puppy's ears, to maintain a relaxed hand, rather than an inwardly pitched "collapsed wrist." Achieving a positive wrist position will set up an aligned entry and good catch (see figure 14).

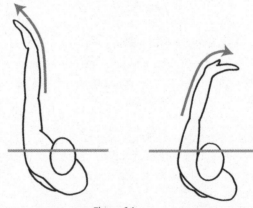

Figure 14:

Pitch your hand outward during
recovery for a well-aligned
entry and good catch.

A "collapsed wrist" leads
to an over-reached entry
and poor catch position.

Rhythmic Breathing – Practicing patterns of breathing in backstroke, including inhale on one stroke, exhale on the other, inhale and exhale during each recovery, and, inhale during one stroke cycle, and exhale on the next, in order to include rhythmic breathing as a regular part of your backstroke.

Roll, Pull/Roll, Push – Regular backstroke feeling that the continuous rolling action provides momentum and leverage to the pull and the push of the arm stroke. Roll down to catch and pull, roll up to transition and push.

Two-Step Recovery – Regular backstroke, practicing an aligned recovery by doing a half recovery, returning in a controlled manner to the starting position, then doing a whole recovery.

Up and Over – Practicing the path of the backstroke arm stroke, where you catch deep then move your hand up and over your stationary elbow, then press the hand past the hip (see figure 15).

Figure 15: Sweep your hand up and over your elbow, past your shoulder.

Vertical Kicking – Stationary flutter kicking in deep water from a vertical position, vigorously enough to keep the face out of the water, to develop a productive kick.

Waterline Drill – Stationary drill where you practice achieving a neutral head position, with the waterline surrounding your face and covering your ears, for best backstroke floating position.

BREASTSTROKE DRILLS

2 Kick Breaststroke – To begin the bridge drill to swim, but to still emphasize that each stroke begins and ends in a streamline position, float in a hand lead position and do three breaststroke kicks in a row, then one complete stroke cycle of arm stroke, breathing, kick and glide, and repeat.

3 Kick Breaststroke – To emphasize that each stroke begins and ends in a streamline position, float in a hand lead position and do three breaststroke kicks in a row, then do one complete stroke cycle of arm stroke, breathing, kick and glide, and repeat.

Breaststroke Alternating Dolphin and Breaststroke Kick – Breaststroke arm stroke with a dolphin as you press out, and another as you sweep in, then a complete breaststroke arm stroke, breath, kick and glide, and repeat, emphasizing the rocking action and core use in the breaststroke, and bridging from drill to swim.

Breaststroke Arms With Flutter Kick – To isolate the arm stroke and breathing and still have the benefit of kick momentum.

Breaststroke Kick on Back – Floating on back, from a head-leading position, do breaststroke kick, trying to touch your heels to your fingertips, while making sure that your knees stay under the water, to produce a straight line from shoulder to knee, thereby eliminating potential kick

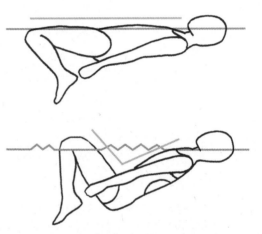

Figure 16: Achieve a straight body position, from shoulder to knee to eliminate drag produced from drawing the knees up and bending at the hip.

Breaststroke With Dolphin – Breaststroke arm stroke with a dolphin as you press out, and another as you sweep in, emphasizing the rocking action and core use in the breaststroke.

Breaststroke With Fists – Breaststroke arm stroke with fists, using the forearms to press against the water to develop a stable, high elbow position on outsweep, and to use the full paddle available on the insweep.

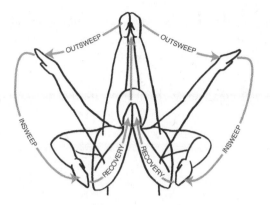

Figure 17: The path of the breaststroke arms underwater.

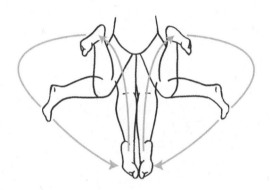

Figure 18: The path of the breaststroke kick.

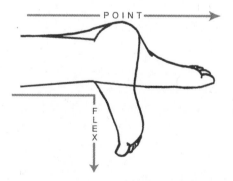

Figure 19: Breaststroke kick requires a full range of foot positions ranging from fully flexed to fully pointed.

Corners Drill – Regular breaststroke, focusing on achieving lift for the breathing without pressing down on the water, but instead, by accelerating from the outsweep into the insweep, and holding on to the water well during the transition from one to the other (see figure 17).

Duck Feet – Stationary drill to practice the continual ankle rotation needed to keep the bottom of the feet pressing against the water at all stages of the power phase of the kick (see figure 18).

Eyes on the Water – Regular breaststroke where you look down at the water while inhaling, rather than forward, in order to continue the forward line of the stroke.

Flex/Point – Stationary drill where you practice alternately flexing and pointing your feet, first while watching your feet and feeling the muscles required, then by just feeling the actions, to achieve the foot positions needed for a productive breaststroke kick (see figure 19).

31

Fold and Shrug - Regular breaststroke where you focus on increasing your momentum into recovery by shrugging your shoulders up as you breathe and finish the insweep, then rolling them down and forward into your quick recovery.

Glide Length, Glide Speed - Regular breaststroke focusing on starting the next stroke at the exact point where to maintain momentum. Too short, and you do not benefit from the glide; too long, and you lose momentum.

Grow Your Recovery - First stationary, then while swimming, practice extending your stroke length by straightening elbows, then by bringing forearms closer together, then by leaning forward into your recovery. Finally, do all at once.

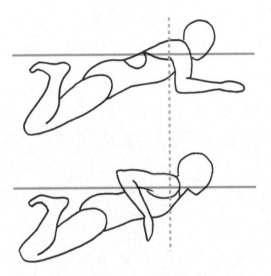

Half Breaststroke - Regular breaststroke progressively reducing the width and depth of the arm stroke so your hands and forearms stay within your rage of sight at all times, avoiding a dropped elbow "chicken wing" position, in order to get the most forward motion, with the least drag (see figure 20).

Figure 20: Keep your arm stroke in front of your chest, with your hands always within your range of sight to produce less drag. Avoid letting your elbows to drop back like chicken wings.

Hand Speed Drill - To practice no pauses in the arm stroke, especially at the "drag point" that can occur at the transition from insweep and recovery, do breaststroke arm stroke with flutter kick, trying to accomplish a complete arm stroke (outsweep, insweep, recovery) within the time it takes to do four flutter kick downbeats, then hold in streamline for six kicks, and continue.

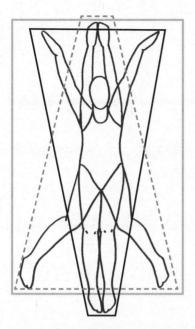

Figure 21: To minimize form drag in the breaststroke: first stroke (black silhouette), then kick (dotted silhouette). Avoid doing both at once (gray silhouette).

Head-Up Breaststroke Arms With Flutter Kick – To be able to isolate the path of the arm stroke, and watch it, while feeling lift in the stroke, and still have the benefit of kick momentum.

Head-Up Breaststroke Kick – Breaststroke kick with your chin on the water's surface, first with hands leading, then with head leading, to practice kick productivity.

Inhale at the High Point – Regular breaststroke where you achieve the breathing position through a combination of the lift from the accelerating arm stroke, and the rocking motion of the stroke, rather than raising the head independently, or pressing down on the water.

No Stars – Regular breaststroke maintaining the sequence "stroke then kick," to avoid producing drag where the stroke cancels out the kick, and the kick cancels out the stroke, when the stroke and kick are done simultaneously. Stroke and then kick, and repeat to achieve stroke timing that will produce the narrowest body position during the power phases of the stroke, and the least drag and width to the stroke (see figure 21).

Rocking Drill – A stationary drill where you alternately rock your head and chest upward as you bend your knees and raise your heels toward your buttocks, then rock your head and chest downward as you straighten your legs, to practice the basic rocking action of the breaststroke.

Sculling – Press out with thumbs down, press in with thumbs up, in order to develop better "feel" for lateral motion of the breaststroke arm stroke.

Shoot to Streamline - Regular breaststroke where you focus on eliminating any pause at the end of the insweep, and accelerating through this "drag point," using your momentum to get back to the streamline position (see figure 22).

Figure 22:

Shoot through the "drag point" to streamline.

Avoid getting stuck in the "drag point."

Streamline - A push off drill to feel the effect of drag and to practice eliminating it, and progressively build an effective breaststroke home base position.

Stroke, Breathe, Kick, Glide Mantra - Regular breaststroke, while saying each stroke element "stroke, breathe, kick, glide" in sequence, as it happens, trying to make the stroke, breathe, kick take up about as much time as the glide by itself.

Stroke Up to Breathe, Kick Down to Glide - Regular breaststroke focusing on using the leverage of the stroke by stroking and breathing while rocking up, and kicking and gliding while rocking down (see figure 23).

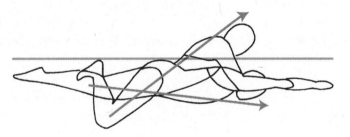

Figure 23: Stroke up to breathe, kick down to glide.

Tennis Ball Drill – Regular breaststroke holding a tennis ball under your chin, to practice maintaining a stable head position for the most productive forward motion.

Thread the Needle – Regular breaststroke where after each stroke you try to make a small hole in the water with your hands, then pass through that same hole with your elbows, shoulders and head, chest, hips, legs and feet, to feel the most streamlined stroke.

Vertical Breaststroke Kick – Stationary breaststroke kick in deep water from a vertical position, vigorously enough to keep the face out of the water, to develop a productive kick.

BUTTERFLY DRILLS

Advanced One-Arm Butterfly – From a head leading position, do butterfly with one arm only, while the other arm remains at your side, to practice butterfly stroke rhythm, the pull and push of the arm stroke, and focus on getting the chest down in a more sustainable manner than the full stroke.

Back Dolphin – First in head leading, then in hand leading position, do dolphin while floating on your back, trying to feel that the power comes from the core. Try to keep your face dry, by keeping your head still.

Body Wave – From a head leading float position, dip the head, then chest and flow this action down to your hips and feet to create fluid wave, and forward motion emphasizing starting the action high in the body (see figure 24).

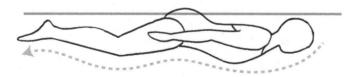

Figure 24: Start your body wave by dipping your head and chest, and let it flow down to your feet.

Bowing – Stationary drill where you stand and bow forward, leaving your hips stationary, and use your abdominal muscles to control the action down and up, to simulate the constant high hips position of the butterfly.

Breaststroke With Dolphin – Breaststroke arm stroke with two dolphins during each arm stroke, emphasizing the core use, constant kick, and rhythm of the butterfly.

Breathing Timing Drill – Stationary drill where you stand in waist-deep water, bend at the hips and lean forward so your face is in the water. With arms extended forward, do an arm stroke, and stand as your arms press toward the back. Breathe in the standing position. Recover and bend forward again, and repeat. Exhale while your face is in the water; inhale when your face clears the water.

Chest Balance – Regular butterfly focusing on the point when your chest is at its lowest point, and you feel as if you are riding downhill and forward for an instant before you start your arm stroke and your chest rises, giving leverage to the stroke that would not be present from a flat body position (see figure 25).

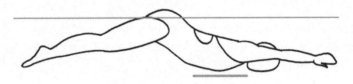

Figure 25: Balance on your chest as you reach for your catch.

Coordination Checkpoint – Regular butterfly focusing on coordinating three actions so they occur at exactly the same time: the round off finish of the underwater arm stroke, the downward snap of the second kick, and the inhale.

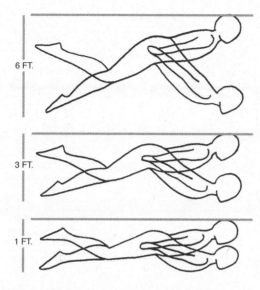

6 FT.

3 FT.

1 FT.

Figure 26: Exaggerate the wave of your dolphin, then gradually reduce it until you feel a compact and productive dolphin action.

Deep to Shallow Dolphin – Head leading dolphin, first passing down and up through six feet of water, then three feet of water, then just one foot of water, to feel a fluid yet compact dolphin (see figure 26).

Dipping – Stationary drill, where you float in a head lead position and practice dipping your chest rhythmically, downward a few inches into the water, then returning to the starting position, and feeling how doing so leads the rest of your body to do follow the action.

Dolphin Dives – In waist-deep water, stand with arms at your sides, then jump up, over, and down into the water, face first. Before your reach the bottom, shift your weight back to a standing position, arms still at your sides and repeat. Emphasizes the full body action of the butterfly (see figure 27).

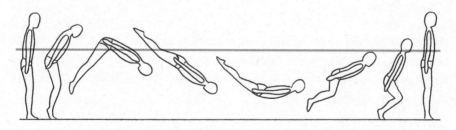

Figure 27: Practice generating butterfly action from the core.

Eyes on the Water Butterfly – Regular butterfly where you look down at the water while inhaling, rather than forward, in order to continue the forward line of the stroke.

Flying Dolphin Dives – In waist-deep water, stand with arms back as if you have just released the water, take a breath and then swing your arms around like the butterfly recovery as you jump up, over, and down into the water, face first. Before your reach the bottom, shift your weight back to a standing position, arms back, and repeat. Emphasizes the full body action of the butterfly and the breathing position.

Freestyle With Dolphin – Regular freestyle arms with a dolphin kick each time your hand strikes the water in front. Notice that the other arm will be finishing the push phase of the arm stroke at the same time. An excellent and sustainable drill for kick timing (see figure 4).

Hammer and Nail – Regular butterfly, breathing each stroke, imagining that your forehead is a hammer and the water is a nail. When your head returns to the water, strike the nail with force. Avoid striking the water with your chin which will lead to frontal drag.

Left Arm, Right Arm, Both Arms – From a hand leading position, do one butterfly stroke with your left arm only, then one with your right arm, then a stroke with both arms. Start each new stroke when the previous stroke returns to the starting point. To practice butterfly stroke rhythm and to bridge from drill to swim.

No-Kick Butterfly – Regular butterfly except consciously do not kick. Keep your hips up and raise and dip your chest, and notice that the kick flows down to your feet anyway. This drill emphasizes initiating the kick from high in the body, rather than from the feet.

No-Pause Butterfly – Also known as "Grab and Go Butterfly", where you swim four to eight strokes of butterfly, with absolutely no hesitation between the extension and the catch, the point momentum is commonly lost. Then finish the length in easy freestyle and repeat.

One-Arm Butterfly – From a hand leading position, do butterfly with one arm only, while the other arm remains extended, to practice butterfly stroke rhythm, the pull and push of the arm stroke, and focus on keeping the hips up in a more sustainable manner than the full stroke.

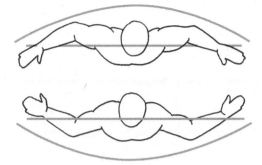

Figure 28: Achieve a positive recovery.
Swing your arms over the water with your pinkies
up so your elbows won't drag through the water.

Pinkies Up – Regular butterfly focusing on maintaining a consistent "pinkie-up" hand position during recovery, so the elbows do not drag through the water, but rather the arms make an arch over the water's surface, accomplishing a "positive recovery" (see figure 28).

Pitch to Press – A stationary drill to practice pressing back on the water, rather than down, and to maintain constant pressure on the water by changing the pitch of your hands throughout the path of the stroke. Stand in waist-deep water, and bend forward until your face is submerged. Start with your hands extended in the butterfly entry position. Do a butterfly arm stroke, pressing out and back, then sweeping in and back, then again pressing out and back, and repeat.

Reaching to a "Y" – Regular butterfly focusing on a wide Y-shaped entry, leading with the thumbs in order to produce the most aligned position to start the stroke, and the best catch position (see figure 29).

Figure 29:

Reach to a "Y" when entering the water to start the power phase from a positionof strength.

Reaching to the middle with collapsed elbows starts the power phase from a position of weakness.

Recovery in Place – Stationary drill standing in chest-deep water, bringing the arms over the water first with the thumbs leading (negative recovery), then again with the thumbs trailing (positive recovery), and repeat to identify the most relaxed recovery arm position, that completely clears the water.

Round-Off – Regular butterfly focusing on finishing the arm stroke by pressing outward, like a "J" from the hips, for easy release from the water, and a quick transition to recovery.

The Flop – Regular butterfly focusing on initiating the recovery from the shoulders, to achieve a relaxed forward reaching recovery. Release the water, pinkies up, swing arms wide and around from the shoulders, not the hands, until your arms are at shoulder level. Then, roll your shoulders forward and redirect your hands to reach forward, and as they do drop your chest into the water.

Tracing Question Marks – Regular butterfly, tracing the path of the butterfly arms, wide to narrow, in order to practice the front to back sweep of the arm stroke (see figure 30).

Vertical Dolphin – Stationary dolphin kick in deep water from a vertical position, vigorously enough to keep the face out of the water, to develop a productive kick.

Figure 30: The path of the butterfly arm stroke underwater.

Weight-Shifting – In a head leading floating position, do a bowing motion, hips constantly high, feeling how your weight shifts forward as you bow down, and back as you bow up, creating leverage and forward motion.

WORKOUTS

TECHNIQUE WORKOUTS FOR FREESTYLE

WORKOUT 1

FOCUS POINT:	Core tension for better body position
Warm-up:	200
Kick:	200 flutter kick
Drill:	4 x 25 Head Lead Kick w/10 SR – Chin down
Drill:	4 x 25 Log Roll w/10 SR – Chin down, roll from hips
Drill:	4 x 25 Head Lead Kick w/10 SR – Chin down
Drill:	4 x 25 12 Kick Switch w/10 SR – Chin down, switch from hips
Drill/Swim:	4 x 50 w/15 SR – 25 drill, 25 swim (Use drills above)
Swim:	4 x 100 Freestyle w/20 SR – Chin down, roll from hips, feel core tension
50 Easy	
Swim:	6 x 25 Freestyle – Fast/Easy w/ 15 SR – maintain core tension on fast 25s
Cool-down:	100
Total:	1,500

WORKOUT 2

FOCUS POINT:	Swim downhill
Warm-up:	200
Drill:	200 Head Lead Kick – Chin down, balance on chest
Swim:	4 x 50 Freestyle w/10 SR – Chin down, balance on chest
Drill:	200 Log Roll – Chin and chest down, roll from hips
Swim:	4 x 50 Freestyle w/10 SR – Chin down, balance on chest, roll from hips
50 Easy	
Pull/Swim:	4 x 100 w/20 SR – Chin down, balance on chest, roll from hips
Swim:	8 x 25 Fast Freestyle w/30 SR – Swim downhill
Cool-down:	100
Total:	1,750

WORKOUT 3

FOCUS POINT:	Your spine is your axis
Warm-up:	200
Kick:	6 x 25 flutter kick w/10 SR
Drill:	4 x 50 12 Kick Switch w/10 SR
Drill:	4 x 50 6 Kick Switch w/10 SR
Drill:	4 x 50 3 Kick Switch w/10 SR
Drill/Swim:	4 x 75 – alternating 50 6 Kick Switch/25 Freestyle w/10 SR
50 Easy	
Pull:	200 Freestyle – roll from hips, feel your axis
Swim:	4 x 50 Freestyle w/15 SR – roll from hips, maintain your axis
Cool-down:	200
Total:	1,800

WORKOUT 4

FOCUS POINT:	Find your line
Warm-up:	200
Drill:	100 12 Kick Switch – Align reaching hand and shoulder
Drill:	100 6 Kick Switch – Align reaching hand, shoulder and hip
Drill:	100 3 Kick Switch – Align reaching hand, shoulder, hip and foot
Swim:	4 x 50 Freestyle w/15 SR – establish your line from finger to toe
Swim:	4 x 50 Freestyle w/15 SR – maintain your line
Swim:	4 x 50 Freestyle w/15 SR – feel your line
50 Easy	
Pull:	200 – Roll from the hip, find your line
Swim:	4 x 25 Fast Freestyle w/10 SR – maintain your line
Pull:	200 – Roll from the hip, feel your line
Cool-down:	100
Total:	1,750

WORKOUT 5

FOCUS POINT:	Effective kicking – Snap down, relax up, point toes
Warm-up:	200
Kick:	200 flutter kick – use pointed toes and floppy ankles
Kick:	4 x 25 w/10 SR – snap foot down, relax up
Kick:	4 x 25 w/10 SR – feel resistance on the top of your foot
Kick:	4 x 25 w/10 SR – use quick, narrow kick
50 Easy	
Swim:	4 x 50 Freestyle w/15 SR – snap foot down, relax up
Swim:	4 x 50 Freestyle w/15 SR – feel resistance on the top of your foot
Swim:	4 x 50 Freestyle w/15 SR – use quick, narrow kick
50 Easy	
Kick:	4 x 25 Fast Kick w/30 SR – keep heels below surface, but make a splash
Swim:	4 x 25 Fast Freestyle w/30 SR – keep heels below surface, but make a splash
Cool-down:	100
Total:	1,700

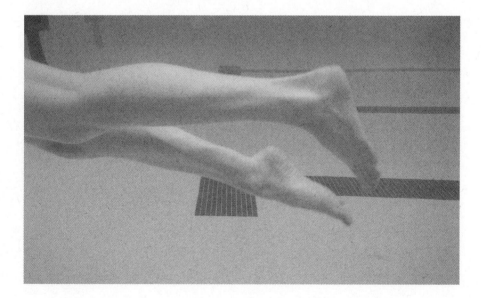

WORKOUT 6

FOCUS POINT:	Fish don't have knees! Develop "fluid kicking"
Warm-up:	200
Kick:	4 x 50 flutter kick w/ 10 SR
Drill:	4 x 25 Underwater Streamline Kick w/15 SR
Kick:	4 x 25 flutter kick w/kickboard – no splash w/15 SR
Swim:	8 x 50 Freestyle w/15 SR – with fluid kick
Drill:	4 x 50 One-Leg Kick w/20 SR (25 left, 25 right)
Kick:	100 flutter kick (both legs)
Swim:	8 x 50 Freestyle w/15 SR – with fluid kick
50 Easy	
Swim:	4 x 25 Fast Freestyle w/15 SR – fast fluid kick
Cool-down:	100
Total:	1,950

WORKOUT 7

FOCUS POINT:	Kick with no blank spots
Warm-up:	200
Kick:	200 flutter kick – alternating 25s w/splash and w/no splash
Drill:	Vertical Kicking – minor sculling with hands – 30 sec. – Keep head above water
Drill:	Vertical Kicking – cross arms over chest – 30 sec. – Keep head above water
Drill:	Vertical Kicking – hands up – 30 sec. – Keep head above water
Drill:	100 3 Strokes, 3 Kicks
Swim:	8 x 50 Freestyle – 6 kicks per arm cycle
Drill:	4 x 50 One-Leg Kick w/20 SR (25 left, 25 right)
Swim:	8 x 50 Freestyle w/15 SR – no blank spots when breathing
Cool-down:	100
Total:	1,600 + 1.5 min. stationary drill

WORKOUT 8

FOCUS POINT:	Swim tall
Warm-up:	200
Kick:	200 flutter kick
Swim:	4 x 25 Freestyle w/10 SR – count your strokes
Drill:	4 x 25 Catch-Up w/10 SR – count your strokes, compare
Drill:	4 x 25 3 Kick Switch w/10 SR – count your strokes, compare
Swim:	4 x 25 Freestyle w/10 SR – count your strokes, compare
Pull:	200 – use full extension each stroke
Swim:	4 x 50 Freestyle w/15 SR – count your stokes
Pull:	200 – roll into and out of each stroke
Swim:	4 x 50 Freestyle w/15 SR – count your stokes, compare
Swim:	4 x 25 Freestyle w/15 SR – swim tall
Cool-down:	100
Total:	1,800

WORKOUT 9

FOCUS POINT:	Extend entry from the elbow
Warm-up:	200
Kick:	200 flutter kick
Swim:	4 x 50 Freestyle w/15 SR – count strokes
Drill:	4 x 50 Catch-up Drill w/10 SR – extend entry from elbow
Swim:	4 x 50 Freestyle w/15 SR – count strokes, compare
Swim:	5 x 100 Freestyle w/15 SR – roll from hips and extend entry from elbow
50 Easy	
Pull:	200 – roll from hips and extend entry from elbow
Cool-down:	100
Total:	1,850

WORKOUT 10

FOCUS POINT:	Feel your paddle
Warm-up:	200
Kick:	200 flutter kick
Drill:	4 x 50 Fist Drill w/10 SR – use forearm as paddle
Swim:	4 x 50 Freestyle w/10 SR – use palm and forearm as paddle
Drill:	4 x 50 Fist Drill w/10 SR – maintain high elbows
Swim:	4 x 50 Freestyle w/10 SR – maintain high elbows
Pull:	300 – use palm and forearm as paddle, maintain high elbows
Swim:	8 x 25 Fast Freestyle w/30 SR – feel your paddle
Cool-down:	100
Total:	1,800

WORKOUT 11

FOCUS POINT:	Point with your thumbs
Warm-up:	200
Kick:	4 x 50 flutter kick w/10 SR
Swim:	6 x 50 Freestyle w/10 SR – count strokes
Drill:	6 x 50 All Thumbs Drill w/10 SR – feel your catch
Swim:	6 x 50 Freestyle w/10 SR – point with thumbs, count strokes, compare
50 Easy	
Pull:	200 – roll from hips, point with thumbs, feel your catch
Swim:	8 x 25 – roll from hips, point with thumbs, feel your catch
Cool-down:	100
Total:	1,850

WORKOUT 12

FOCUS POINT:	Anchor your hand
Warm-up:	200
Kick:	200 flutter kick
Drill:	100 Sculling – hold on to the water
Swim:	4 x 50 Freestyle w/10 SR – extend from elbow
Swim:	4 x 50 Freestyle w/10 SR – positive wrist position
Swim:	4 x 50 Freestyle w/10 SR – pitch hand to enter thumb side
Swim:	4 x 50 Freestyle w/10 SR – roll from hips
Swim:	4 x 50 Freestyle w/10 SR – point with thumbs
Swim:	4 x 50 Freestyle w/10 SR – catch from pinkie side
50 Easy	
Swim:	4 x 50 Freestyle w/10 SR – combine all the above to anchor your hand
Cool-down:	100
Total:	1,950

WORKOUT 13

FOCUS POINT:	Pull then push
Warm-up:	200
Kick:	200 flutter kick
Drill:	3 x 100 Pull/Push Freestyle w/15 SR – pull from full extension to shoulder
Drill:	3 x 100 Pull/Push Freestyle w/15 SR – push from shoulder past hip
50 Easy	
Swim:	4 x 50 Freestyle w/10 SR – feel pull, then push
Pull:	200 – roll from hips, feel pull, then push
Swim:	4 x 50 Freestyle w/10 SR – roll from hips, feel pull, and push
50 Easy	
Swim:	4 x 25 Fast Freestyle w/15 SR – feel pull, then push in each stroke
Cool-down:	100
Total:	1,900

WORKOUT 14

FOCUS POINT:	Stroke front to back
Warm-up:	200
Kick:	200 flutter kick
Drill:	200 – your choice
Swim:	4 x 100 Freestyle w/15 SR – pull back, avoid pressing down
Swim:	4 x 100 Freestyle w/15 SR – push back, avoid lifting up
Drill:	4 x 50 One-Arm Freestyle – pull back, push back
Swim:	4 x 50 Freestyle – stroke front to back
Cool-down:	100
Total:	1,900

WORKOUT 15

FOCUS POINT:	Benefit from the pendulum effect
Warm-up:	200
Kick:	4 x 50 underwater streamline flutter kick
Drill:	4 x 50 Shark Fin w/10 SR
Swim:	4 x 50 Freestyle w/10 SR – high elbow recovery, low opposite hip
Drill:	4 x 50 Shark Fin w/10 SR
Swim:	4 x 50 Freestyle w/10 SR – high elbow recovery, low opposite hip
50 Easy	
Drill:	100 Pendulum – high elbow recovery, low opposite hip
Pull:	200 – feel the pendulum rhythm
Swim:	3 x 100 Freestyle – high elbow recovery, low opposite hip, pendulum rhythm
Cool-down:	100
Total:	1,950

WORKOUT 16

FOCUS POINT:	Relax your hand during recovery
Warm-up:	200
Kick:	4 x 25 Fast flutter kick w/10 SR
Drill:	100 – your choice
Swim:	4 x 50 Freestyle w/10 SR – elbow higher than hand for entire recovery
Drill:	4 x 50 Floppy Hand Drill w/10 SR
Swim:	4 x 50 Freestyle w/10 SR – floppy hand, elbow higher than hand
Drill:	4 x 50 Shark Fin w/10 SR – elbow high, fingers pointed back toward feet
Swim:	4 x 50 Freestyle w/10 SR – fingers pointed back toward feet
50 Easy	
Drill:	200 Pendulum – with floppy hand and fingers pointed back toward feet
Pull:	200 – feel your floppy hand
Cool-down:	100
Total:	1,950

WORKOUT 17

FOCUS POINT:	Rest during recovery
Warm-up:	200
Kick:	200 flutter kick
Drill:	200 – your choice
Drill:	100 3 Strokes, 6 Kicks
Drill:	100 Shark Fin
Pull:	200 – roll from hips, feel pendulum
Swim:	8 x 50 Freestyle w/10 SR – roll from hips, rest recovering arm
50 Easy	
Swim:	8 x 25 Freestyle w/15 SR – rest recovering arm
50 Easy	
Swim:	8 x 25 Fast Freestyle w/15 SR – rest recovering arm
Cool-down:	100
Total:	2,000

WORKOUT 18

FOCUS POINT:	Breathe from the hip
Warm-up:	200
Kick:	4 x 50 flutter kick w/10 SR
Drill:	200 3 Strokes, 6 Kicks
Swim:	4 x 50 Freestyle w/10 SR – keep chin aligned with breastbone
Swim:	4 x 50 Freestyle w/10 SR – roll from hip to breathe
Drill:	4 x 50 Dead-Arm Freestyle, alternating 50s of left arm stroking/ right arm stroking w/15 SR – chin aligned with breastbone, roll hips to breathe
Swim:	4 x 50 Freestyle w/10 SR – keep chin aligned with breastbone
50 Easy	
Swim:	4 x 50 Freestyle w/10 SR – roll from hip to breathe
50 Easy	
Swim:	4 x 50 Freestyle w/10 SR – bilateral breathing
Cool-down:	100
Total:	2,000

WORKOUT 19

FOCUS POINT:	Low profile breathing
Warm-up:	200
Kick:	100 flutter kick
Drill:	100 – your choice
Kick:	100 flutter kick
Swim:	4 x 50 Freestyle w/10 SR – feel cheek connected to water when breathing
Swim:	4 x 50 Freestyle w/10 SR – feel jawbone connected to water when breathing
Swim:	4 x 50 Freestyle w/10 SR – feel temple connected to water when breathing
Swim:	4 x 50 Freestyle w/10 SR – feel all the above connected to water when breathing
Pull:	200 – press temple into the water when breathing
Drill:	4 x 25 12 Kick Switch w/10 SR – press temple into the water when breathing
Drill:	4 x 25 Dead-Arm Freestyle w/10 SR – alternating 25s of left/right) – press temple
Swim:	4 x 50 Freestyle w/10 SR – with low profile breathing
Cool-down:	100
Total:	2,000

WORKOUT 20

FOCUS POINT:	Develop a weightless reaching hand
Warm-up:	200
Kick:	200 flutter kick
Drill:	200 12 Kick Switch – find your line
Drill:	200 6 Kick Switch – feel your line
Drill:	200 3 Kick Switch – maintain your line
Swim:	4 x 50 Freestyle w/10 SR – maintain line while breathing
50 Easy	
Drill:	200 Catch-Up Drill – feel line while breathing
Drill:	200 Pendulum – high recovering elbow, low opposite hip while breathing
Swim:	4 x 50 Freestyle w/10 SR – achieve the weightless hand while breathing
Cool-down:	100
Total:	1,950

WORKOUT 21

FOCUS POINT:	Skate on your hips
Warm-up:	200
Kick:	200 flutter kick
Swim:	100 Freestyle – count strokes
Drill:	4 x 100 Hip Skating w/15 SR
Pull:	4 x 100 w/15 SR – skating on hips
Swim:	4 x 100 Freestyle w/15 SR – skating on hips
50 Easy	
Swim:	100 Freestyle – skating on hips, count strokes, compare
Cool-down:	100
Total:	1,950

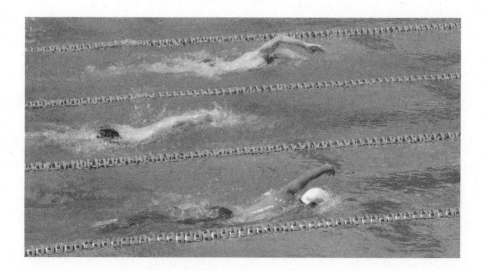

WORKOUT 22

FOCUS POINT:	Use your dominant kick
Warm-up:	200
Kick:	8 x 25 flutter kick w/10 SR
Swim:	4 x 50 Freestyle w/10 SR – no blank spots in kick
Drill:	4 x 25 Head-Up Freestyle w/15 SR – kick down as hand strikes the water in front
Drill:	4 x 50 Freestyle With Dolphin w/10 SR – kick down as hand strikes the water in front
Swim:	4 x 50 Freestyle w/10 SR – kick down as hand strikes the water in front
Drill:	4 x 50 Freestyle With Dolphin w/10 SR – faster tempo, same coordination
Swim:	4 x 50 Freestyle w/10 SR – faster tempo, same coordination
50 Easy	
Drill/Swim:	12 x 25 w/30 SR – alternating 25s of Fast Freestyle With Dolphin/Fast Freestyle
Cool-down:	100
Total:	1,950

WORKOUT 23

FOCUS POINT:	Feel the water
Warm-up:	200
Kick:	200 flutter kick
Drill:	200 your choice
Drill:	4 x 50 Sculling w/10 SR – arms extended
Drill:	4 x 50 Sculling w/10 SR – arms at ribs
Drill:	4 x 50 Sculling w/10 SR – arms at hips
Swim:	3 x 100 Freestyle w/15 SR – feel on to water
50 Easy	
Swim:	2 x 100 Freestyle w/15 SR – hold on to the water
50 Easy	
Swim:	1 x 100 Fast Freestyle – maintain hold on the water
Cool-down:	100
Total:	2,000

WORKOUT 24

FOCUS POINT:	Feel core-centered swimming
Warm-up:	200
Kick:	200 flutter kick
Drill:	100 Log Roll – initiate roll from hips
Drill:	100 Dead-Arm Freestyle – initiate roll from hips
Drill:	100 Pendulum – find line on each stroke
Swim:	4 x 25 Freestyle w/10 SR – count strokes
Swim:	4 x 50 Freestyle w/10 SR – roll into and out of each stroke
Pull:	200 – roll into and out of each stroke
Swim:	4 x 50 Freestyle w/10 SR – hips and shoulders roll together
Pull:	200 – hips and shoulders roll together
Swim:	4 x 50 Freestyle w/10 SR – feel unified core action
Swim:	4 x 25 Fast Freestyle w/10 SR – roll becomes a snap, count strokes, compare
Cool-down:	100
Total:	2,000

WORKOUT 25

FOCUS POINT:	Find your best breathing rhythm
Warm-up:	200
Kick:	8 x 25 flutter kick w/10 SR
Drill:	200 Dead-Arm Freestyle – alternate lengths of left arm/right arm
Swim:	200 Freestyle – breathe facing the same side of the pool the whole time
Swim:	4 x 50 Freestyle w/10 SR – breathe every 2 strokes
Swim:	4 x 50 Freestyle w/10 SR – breathe every 3 strokes
Swim:	4 x 50 Freestyle w/10 SR – breathe every 4 strokes
Swim:	4 x 50 Freestyle w/10 SR – breathe every 5 strokes
Swim:	4 x 50 Freestyle w/10 SR – your choice of breathing pattern
Swim:	4 x 25 Fast Freestyle w/30 SR – same breathing pattern, roll into and out of each breath
Cool-down:	100
Total:	2,000

TECHNIQUE WORKOUTS FOR BACKSTROKE

WORKOUT **26**

FOCUS POINT:	Freestyle – backstroke contrast
Warm-up:	200
Kick:	8 x 25 alternating on front/on back w/10 SR – hands leading
Drill:	4 x 50 alternating 50s of Freestyle 12 Kick Switch/ Backstroke 12 Kick Switch w/15 SR – roll from hips
Swim:	4 x 50 alternating 25s of Freestyle/Backstroke w/15 SR – feel similar roll from hips
Drill:	4 x 50 alternating 50s of Freestyle 6 Kick Switch/ Backstroke 6 Kick Switch w/15 SR – swim tall
Swim:	4 x 50 alternating 25s of Freestyle/Backstroke w/15 SR – feel similar alignment
Drill:	4 x 50 Fist Drill alternating 50s of front/back w/15 SR – use forearm as paddle
Swim:	4 x 50 alternating 25s of Freestyle/Backstroke w/15 SR – feel similar paddle
Cool-down:	100
Total:	1,700

WORKOUT 27

FOCUS POINT:	Float on your spine
Warm-up:	200
Kick:	200 alternating 25s on front/back
Drill:	Float on Spine – 1 min.
Kick:	4 x 25 on back w/10 SR – head leading, float on spine
Kick:	4 x 25 on back w/10 SR – hands leading, float on spine
Drill:	Waterline Drill – 1 min.
Kick:	4 x 25 on back w/10 SR – head leading, good waterline
Kick:	4 x 25 on back w/10 SR – hands leading, good waterline
Kick/Swim:	8 x 50 Alternating 25s of kicking on back/backstroke w/15 SR
Swim:	8 x 50 Backstroke w/15 SR – float on spine, good waterline
Cool-down:	100
Total:	1,700 + 2 min. stationary drills

WORKOUT 28

FOCUS POINT:	Feel the banana position
Warm-up:	200
Kick:	200 your choice
Drill:	Float on Spine – 1 min. – contract abdominals as if doing a crunch
Drill:	Waterline Drill – 1 min. – contract abdominals as if doing a crunch
Kick:	4 x 25 on back w/10 SR – head leading – contract abdominals, achieve the banana position
Kick:	4 x 25 on back w/10 SR – hands leading – contract abdominals, achieve the banana position
Kick/Swim:	4 x 50 backstroke alternating 25s of kick and swim w/15 SR – contract abdominals
Kick/Swim:	4 x 50 backstroke alternating 25s of kick and swim w/15 SR – achieve the banana position
50 Easy	
Drill:	4 x 50 Backstroke 12 Kick Switch – contract abdominals, achieve the banana position
Drill/Swim:	4 x 50 alternating 25s of 12 Kick Switch/Backstroke w/15 SR – maintain the banana position
Swim:	8 x 25 Backstroke w/15 SR – maintain contracted abdominals and the banana position
Cool-down:	100
Total:	1,750 + 2 min. stationary drills

WORKOUT 29

FOCUS POINT:	Achieve a neutral head and relaxed neck
Warm-up:	200
Kick:	200 alternating 25s on back/front
Drill:	4 x 50 Backstroke 12 Kick Switch w/15 SR
Kick:	4 x 25 on back w/10 SR – head leading – achieve good waterline, neutral head position
Kick:	4 x 25 on back w/10 SR – head leading – use water as a pillow, achieve a relaxed neck
Drill:	4 x 50 Backstroke 12 Kick Switch w/15 SR – achieve a neutral head, relaxed neck
Swim:	8 x 50 Backstroke w/15 SR – maintain a neutral head, relaxed neck
50 Easy	
Swim:	8 x 25 alternating 25s of Backstroke/Freestyle w/15 SR – achieve a neutral head, relaxed neck
Cool-down:	100
Total:	1,750

WORKOUT 30

FOCUS POINT:	Feel an "independent head"
Warm-up:	200
Kick:	4 x 50 your choice w/10 SR
Drill:	4 x 50 Backstroke 12 Kick Switch w/15 SR – neutral head position, relaxed neck
Swim:	4 x 50 Backstroke w/15 SR – maintain a neutral head position, relaxed neck
Kick:	4 x 25 on back – head leading w/10 SR – cup on forehead w/ 10 SR – neutral head position Kick: 4 x 25 on back – head leading w/10 SR – cup on forehead w/10 SR – relaxed neck
Drill:	4 x 25 Cup on Forehead – Quarter Turn w/15 SR – neutral head position, relaxed neck
50 Easy	
Drill:	4 x 25 Cup on Forehead – Quarter Turn w/15 SR – achieve an "independent head"
Swim:	4 x 50 Backstroke w/15 SR – achieve an "independent head"
Drill:	4 x 50 Cup on Forehead – Quarter Turn w/15 SR – achieve an "independent head"
Swim:	4 x 25 Backstroke w/15 SR – achieve an "independent head"
Cool-down:	100
Total:	1,850

WORKOUT 31

FOCUS POINT:	Getting comfortable on your back
Warm-up:	200
Kick:	200 your choice
Drill:	4 x 50 Backstroke 12 Kick Switch w/10 SR – focus on alignment from reaching arm to feet
Swim:	4 x 25 Backstroke w/10 SR – focus on alignment from reaching arm to feet
Kick:	4 x 25 backstroke kick w/10 SR – notice pool markers such as flags, lane lines
Swim:	4 x 50 Backstroke w/15 SR – use pool markers to gauge distance from wall and direction
Kick:	4 x 25 backstroke kick w/10 SR – head leading – scan for other landmarks such trees or light poles
Kick:	4 x 25 backstroke kick w/10 SR – arms leading – locate same markers as above
Swim:	4 x 50 Backstroke w/15 SR – maintain visual contact with markers
50 Easy	
Kick:	4 x 25 backstroke kick – hands leading – lean slightly to left for 12 kicks; repeat on the right
Kick:	4 x 25 backstroke kick – hands leading – kick 24 kicks then locate marker; lean left or right to steer
Swim:	100 Backstroke – use pool markers and landmarks. Correct direction by leaning to steer.
Cool-down:	100
Total:	1,850

WORKOUT 32

FOCUS POINT:	Productive kicking
Warm-up:	200
Kick:	200 your choice
Drill:	4 x 25 No Knees Streamline Kick w/10 SR
Swim:	4 x 50 Backstroke w/15 SR – keep knees underwater
Drill:	4 x 25 Boiling Water Drill w/10 SR
Swim:	4 x 50 Backstroke w/15 SR – kick water upward
Drill:	4 x 25 Backstroke 12 Kick Switch w/10 SR – focus on quick kicking
Swim:	4 x 50 Backstroke w/15 SR – focus on quick kicking
50 Easy	
Kick:	100 Backstroke Kick – knees underwater, kick water upward, quick kicking
Swim:	100 Backstroke – knees underwater, kick water upward, quick kicking
Swim:	8 x 25 Backstroke w/10 SR – focus on productive kicking
Cool-down:	100
Total:	1,850

WORKOUT 33

FOCUS POINT:	Develop good foot position
Warm-up:	200
Kick:	200 your choice
Drill:	Vertical Kicking – 30 sec. – point toes, feel pressure of water on top of foot
Drill:	Vertical Kicking – 30 sec. – without pointing toes, notice it is difficult to keep your head up
Drill:	Vertical Kicking – 30 sec. – point toes, feel pressure of water on top of foot
50 Easy	
Kick:	100 Backstroke Kick – hands leading – press water upward with top of foot
Kick:	100 Backstroke Kick – hands leading – relax foot as heel drops down
Kick:	100 Backstroke Kick – hands leading – snap foot up, and relaxing it down
50 Easy	
Swim:	4 x 50 Backstroke w/15 SR – snap foot up, relax it down.
Drill:	Vertical Kicking – 30 sec. – toes pointing outward
Drill:	Vertical Kicking – 30 sec. – toes pointing straight down
Drill:	Vertical Kicking – 30 sec. – pigeon-toe position
50 Easy	
Drill:	8 x 25 Pigeon-Toed Kicking w/10 SR
Swim:	4 x 50 Backstroke w/15 SR – use pointed, pigeon-toe foot, snap foot up, relax it down
50 Easy	
Kick/Swim:	4 x 50 alternating 25s of Backstroke Kick/Backstroke w/ 15 SR – use good foot position
Cool-down:	100
Total:	1,800 + 3 min. stationary drills

WORKOUT 34

FOCUS POINT:	Kick with power
Warm-up:	200
Kick:	100 your choice
Kick:	4 x 25 your choice – fast kick w/10 SR
Drill:	4 x 25 No Knees Streamline Kick w/10 SR
Drill:	4 x 25 Pigeon-Toed Kicking w/10 SR
Drill:	4 x 25 Boiling Water Drill w/10 SR
Kick/Swim:	8 x 50 kick on back/Backstroke – use good foot position and productive kick
50 Easy	
Drill:	4 x 25 No Knees Streamline Kick w/10 SR
Drill:	4 x 25 Pigeon-Toed Kicking w/10 SR
Drill:	4 x 25 Boiling Water Drill w/10 SR
Kick/Swim:	6 x 50 alternating 25s of Backstroke Kick/Backstroke – use narrow, quick kicks
50 Easy	
Swim:	4 x 25 Backstroke w/10 SR – use narrow, quick kicks and good foot position for kick power
Cool-down:	100
Total:	1,900

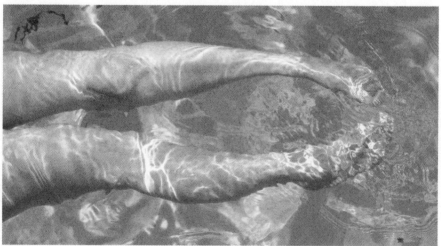

WORKOUT 35

FOCUS POINT:	Feeling the path of the stroke
Warm-up:	200
Kick:	200 your choice
Swim:	200 Freestyle – focus on the straight arm beginning and end of the stroke
Swim:	200 Freestyle – focus on the bent elbow position in the mid-pull
Drill:	4 x 25 One-Arm Rope Climb w/10 SR
Swim:	100 Backstroke – focus on the straight arm beginning and end of the stroke
Swim:	100 Backstroke – focus on the bent elbow position in the mid-pull
Swim:	200 Freestyle – focus on the sweeping path of the stroke
Swim:	200 Freestyle – focus on accelerating toward the end of the stroke
Drill:	4 x 25 Up and Over w/10 SR
Swim:	100 Backstroke – focus on the sweeping path of the stroke
Swim:	100 Backstroke – focus on accelerating towards the end of the stroke
Swim:	4 x 25 Backstroke w/10 SR – feel the path of the stroke
Cool-down:	100
Total:	2,000

WORKOUT 36

FOCUS POINT:	Pull, then push
Warm-up:	200
Kick:	6 x 50 alternating 25s on front/on back
Drill:	100 Pull/Push Freestyle – focus on feeling the pull
Drill:	100 One-Arm Pull/Push Backstroke – focus on feeling the pull
Swim:	200 alternating 25s of Freestyle/Backstroke – focus on feeling the pull
Drill:	100 Pull/Push Freestyle – focus on feeling the push
Drill:	100 One-Arm Pull/Push Backstroke – focus on feeling the push
Swim:	200 alternating 25s of Freestyle/Backstroke – focus on feeling the push
Drill:	100 Pull/Push Freestyle – feel the transition from pull to push
Drill:	100 One-Arm Pull/Push Backstroke – feel the transition from pull to push
Swim:	200 alternating 25s of Freestyle/Backstroke – feel the transition from pull to push
50 Easy	
Swim:	6 x 25 Backstroke w/10 SR – feel pull, then push
Cool-down:	100
Total:	2,000

WORKOUT 37

FOCUS POINT:	Hold on to water
Warm-up:	200
Kick:	6 x 50 – alternating 25s on front/on back
Swim:	200 – alternating 25s of Freestyle/Backstroke – feel the path of the stroke
Swim:	200 – alternating 25s of Freestyle/Backstroke – feel pull, then push
Swim:	200 Backstroke – feel the path of the stroke, and pull, then push
Drill/Swim:	8 x 25 w/10 SR – alternating Fist Backstroke/Backstroke
Drill/Swim:	8 x 25 w/10 SR – alternating One-Arm Pull/Push Backstroke/Backstroke
Swim:	200 Backstroke – hold on to the water throughout the stroke
50 Easy	
Swim:	6 x 25 Backstroke w/10 SR – hold on to the water throughout the stroke
Cool-down:	100
Total:	2,000

WORKOUT 38

FOCUS POINT:	Make a clean hand entry
Warm-up:	200
Kick:	8 x 50 – alternating 50s on front/on back
Swim:	4 x 50 Backstroke w/15 SR – identify what part of your hand enters the water first
Drill:	200 One-Arm Pull/Push Backstroke – enter the water with your pinkie
Swim:	4 x 50 Backstroke w/15 SR – enter the water with your pinkie
50 Easy	
Drill:	200 Backstroke 12 Kick Switch – slice the water with your pinkie at entry
Swim:	4 x 50 Backstroke w/15 SR – slice the water with your pinkie at entry
50 Easy	
Swim:	8 x 25 Backstroke w/10 SR – making a clean hand entry
Cool-down:	100
Total:	2,000

WORKOUT 39

FOCUS POINT:	Catch deep
Warm-up:	200
Kick:	6 x 25 on back w/10 SR
Kick:	6 x 25 on front w/10 SR
Drill:	200 Backstroke 12 Kick Switch – allow reaching hand to descend about 12 inches under the surface
Swim:	4 x 50 Backstroke w/15 SR – allow reaching hand to descend 12 inches under the surface
Drill:	200 One-Arm Pull/Push Backstroke – achieve catch about 12 inches under the surface
Swim:	4 x 50 Backstroke w/15 SR – achieve catch about 12 inches under the surface
Drill:	200 Up and Over – pull upward after your deep catch
Swim:	4 x 50 Backstroke w/15 SR – pull upward after your deep catch
Drill/Swim:	100 alternating 25s of Corkscrew/Backstroke – feel a deep catch each stroke on back
Swim:	4 x 25 Backstroke w/10 SR – catch deep
Cool-down:	100
Total:	2,000

WORKOUT 40

FOCUS POINT:	Entry alignment
Warm-up:	200
Kick:	300 your choice
Drill:	100 Clock Arms – hands enter at 12:00
Drill:	100 Clock Arms – hands enter at 11:00/1:00
Drill:	100 Clock Arms – hands enter at 10:00/2:00
Swim:	200 Backstroke – hands enter between 11:00 /1:00 – 10:00/2:00
Drill:	100 Backstroke 12 Kick Switch – align entering hand with head
Drill:	100 Backstroke 12 Kick Switch – align entering hand with shoulder
Drill:	100 Backstroke 12 Kick Switch – align entering hand outside shoulder
Swim:	200 Backstroke – hands enter aligned with or outside shoulder
Swim:	4 x 50 Backstroke w/10 SR – place hands precisely beyond 12:00 at entry
Swim:	4 x 25 Freestyle w/10 SR
Swim:	4 x 50 Backstroke w/10 SR – place hands precisely at shoulder width or wider at entry
Cool-down:	100
Total:	2,000

WORKOUT 41

FOCUS POINT:	Elbows and alignment
Warm up:	200
Kick:	8 x 50 – alternating 50s on front/on back
Swim:	4 x 50 Backstroke w/15 SR – count strokes
Drill:	4 x 50 Backstroke 12 Kick Switch w/15 SR – firm elbow throughout recovery
Swim:	4 x 50 Backstroke w/15 SR – firm elbow throughout recovery, count strokes, compare
50 Easy	
Swim:	4 x 50 Backstroke w/15 SR – count strokes
Drill:	4 x 50 Locked Elbow Recovery Drill w/15 SR – locked elbow throughout recovery
Swim:	4 x 50 Backstroke w/15 SR – locked elbow throughout recovery, count strokes, compare
Cool-down:	100
Total:	1,950

WORKOUT 42

FOCUS POINT:	Relaxing your hand during recovery
Warm-up:	200
Kick:	200 on front
Kick:	200 on back
Drill:	100 Backstroke 12 Kick Switch – roll from core
Swim:	200 Backstroke – roll from core
Drill:	100 Backstroke 12 Kick Switch – roll from core, relax recovering hand
Swim:	200 Backstroke – roll from core, relax recovering hand
Drill:	100 Two-Step Recovery – stabilize from core
Swim:	200 Backstroke – stabilize from core
Drill:	100 Backstroke 12 Kick Switch – stabilize from core, relax recovering hand
Swim:	200 Backstroke – stabilize from core, relax recovering hand
Swim:	4 x 25 Fast Backstroke w/15 SR – recover with relaxed hands
Cool-down:	100
Total:	1,950

WORKOUT 43

FOCUS POINT:	Avoid a collapsed wrist
Warm-up:	200
Kick:	200 your choice
Drill:	100 Backstroke 12 Kick Switch – switch from core, recovering with shoulders aligned
Drill:	100 Locked Elbow Drill – generate recovery from core, keep elbows locked
Swim:	100 Backstroke – shoulders aligned, elbows locked
Swim:	100 Backstroke – shoulders aligned, elbows locked, positive wrist position
Swim:	4 x 50 Backstroke w/15 SR – count strokes
Drill:	4 x 50 Puppy Ears w/15 SR – positive wrist position
Swim:	4 x 50 Backstroke w/15 SR – positive wrist position – count strokes, compare
Drill:	4 x 50 One-Arm Pull/Push Backstroke w/15 SR – pitch hand outward at entry
Swim:	4 x 50 Backstroke w/15 SR – pitch hand outward at entry – count strokes, compare
Swim:	4 x 25 Fast Backstroke w/15 SR – avoid a collapsed wrist
Cool-down:	100
Total:	2,000

WORKOUT 44

FOCUS POINT:	Opposition
Warm-up:	200
Kick:	8 x 25 on back w/10 SR – alternating 25s fast/medium
Drill:	200 Backstroke 12 Kick Switch – observe relationship between arms
Swim:	200 Backstroke – observe relationship between arms
Drill:	200 Opposition Freeze Frame – notice opposite arm positions
Swim:	200 Backstroke – notice opposite arm positions
Swim:	4 x 50 Backstroke w/15 SR – notice opposition at start and end of stroke
Swim:	4 x 25 Fast Backstroke w/15 SR – maintain opposition
50 Easy	
Swim:	4 x 50 Backstroke w/15 SR – notice opposition in middle of stroke
Swim:	4 x 25 Fast Backstroke w/15 SR – maintain opposition
Cool-down:	100
Total:	1,950

WORKOUT 45

FOCUS POINT:	Using core leverage
Warm-up:	200
Kick:	200 your choice
Drill:	200 Backstroke 12 Kick Switch – feel core stability on each side
Drill/Swim:	200 alternating 25s of Backstroke 12 Kick Switch/ Backstroke – feel core stability on each side
Drill:	200 Backstroke 3 Stroke Switch – feel switch from core
Drill/Swim:	200 alternating 25s of Backstroke 3 Kick Switch/ Backstroke – feel switch from core
Drill:	200 One-Arm Pull/Push – roll into and out of each stroke Drill/
Swim:	200 alternating 25s of One-Arm Pull/Push Backstroke/ Backstroke – roll into and out of each stroke
Swim:	4 x 50 Backstroke w/15 SR – use core to stabilize and roll into and out of each stroke
Swim:	4 x 25 Backstroke w/10 SR – maintain core leverage
Cool-down:	100
Total:	2,000

WORKOUT 46

FOCUS POINT:	Breathing rhythms
Warm-up:	200
Kick:	200 – your choice
Drill:	4 x 25 Breathing Pocket w/10 SR
Swim:	6 x 50 Backstroke w/15 SR – find breathing pocket in each stroke cycle
Drill:	4 x 25 Rhythmic Breathing w/10 SR
Swim:	6 x 50 Backstroke w/15 SR – establish rhythmic breathing
Swim:	25 Backstroke – 10 SR
Swim:	50 Backstroke – 15 SR
Swim:	75 Backstroke – 20 SR
Swim:	100 Backstroke – 25 SR
Swim:	200 Backstroke
Swim:	8 x 25 alternating 25s of Freestyle/Backstroke w/10 SR – use rhythmic breathing
50 Easy	
Swim:	4 x 25 Fast Backstroke w/15 SR – maintain rhythmic breathing
Cool-down:	100
Total:	2,000

WORKOUT 47

FOCUS POINT:	Coordinated backstroke
Warm-up:	200
Kick:	300 – alternating 25s on front/on back
Swim:	50 Backstroke – focus on spine axis
Swim:	50 Backstroke – focus on productive kicking
Swim:	50 Backstroke – focus on good catch
Swim:	50 Backstroke – focus on pull and push
Swim:	50 Backstroke – focus on relaxed, aligned recovery
Swim:	50 Backstroke – focus on rolling from the core
Swim:	100 Backstroke – try to incorporate all of the above
Drill:	200 Armpit Lift
Drill/Swim:	200 alternating 25s of Armpit Lift/Backstroke
Swim:	100 Backstroke – notice how lifting armpit affects stroking arm
Drill:	200 Roll/Pull, Roll/Push
Drill/Swim:	200 alternating 25s of Roll/Pull, Roll/Push/Backstroke
Swim:	100 Backstroke – notice actions on one side of the stroke balance the other side
Cool-down:	100
Total:	2,000

WORKOUT 48

FOCUS POINT:	Backstroke balance
Warm-up:	200
Kick:	100 on back
Kick:	100 on front
Kick:	100 on back
Drill:	100 Cup on Forehead – Quarter Turn – rolling from core
Drill:	100 Cup on Forehead – Quarter Turn – rolling from core, establish an independent head
Swim:	200 Backstroke – rolling from core, maintain an independent head
Drill:	100 Backstroke Balance Drill With Cup – rolling from core, independent head
Drill:	100 Backstroke Balance Drill With Cup – rolling from core, independent head
Swim:	200 Backstroke – rolling from core, independent head, balanced stroke
50 Easy	
Swim:	10 x 50 alternating 50s of Freestyle/Backstroke w/ 15 SR – maintain stroke balance
Cool-down:	100
Total:	1,950

WORKOUT 49

FOCUS POINT:	Constant motion
Warm-up:	200
Kick:	200 – your choice
Drill:	4 x 50 Backstroke 12 Kick Switch w/15 SR
Swim:	4 x 50 Backstroke w/15 SR – no blank spots in kick
Drill:	4 x 50 Backstroke 3 Stroke Switch w/15 SR
Swim:	4 x 50 Backstroke w/15 SR – no flat spots in roll
Drill:	4 x 50 Roll, Pull/Roll, Push w/15 SR
Swim:	4 x 50 Backstroke w/15 SR – no still spots in stroke
50 Easy	
Swim:	8 x 25 Fast Backstroke w/15 SR – constant kick, roll, motion
Cool-down:	100
Total:	1,950

WORKOUT 50

FOCUS POINT:	Freestyle/Backstroke stroke count comparison
Warm-up:	200
Kick:	200 alternating 25s on front/on back
Drill:	200 Freestyle 12 Kick Switch
Drill:	200 Backstroke 12 Kick Switch
Drill/Swim:	200 alternating 25s of Freestyle 12 Kick Switch/ Backstroke 12 Kick Switch
Swim:	200 alternating 25s of Freestyle/Backstroke
Swim:	4 x 50 Freestyle w/10 SR – get average stroke count per 25
Swim:	4 x 50 Backstroke w/10 SR – get average stroke count per 25, compare
Drill:	4 x 25 Corkscrew w/15 SR – feel one stroke freestyle and one stroke backstroke
Swim:	8 x 25 alternating 25s of Freestyle/Backstroke w/15 SR – strive for same stroke count
Cool-down:	100
Total:	2,000

TECHNIQUE WORKOUTS FOR BREASTSTROKE

WORKOUT 51

FOCUS POINT:	Breaststroke's home base position
Warm-up:	200
Kick:	200 – other than breaststroke kick
Drill:	Streamline – 5 minutes
Drill:	200 3 Kick Breaststroke – maintain streamline upper body throughout 3 kick phase
Drill:	200 2 Kick Breaststroke – return to full streamline position after each kick
Swim:	100 Breaststroke – strike streamline position after each kick
Drill:	200 Breaststroke Arms With Flutter Kick – return to full streamline position after each arm stroke
Drill:	200 Head-Up Breaststroke With Flutter Kick – hold streamline position after each arm stroke
Swim:	100 Breaststroke – strike streamline position after each kick
Swim:	4 x 25 Breaststroke w/10 SR – return to home base for 3 seconds after each stroke cycle
Swim:	4 x 25 Breaststroke w/10 SR – return to home base for 2 seconds after each stroke cycle
Cool-down:	100
Total:	1,700 + 5 min. stationary drills

WORKOUT 52

FOCUS POINT:	Breaststroke balance point
Warm-up:	200
Kick:	200 – other than breaststroke kick
Drill:	Rocking Drill – 1 min. – find the "chest high" position at the beginning of each kick
Drill:	Rocking Drill – 1 min. – find the "chest low" position at the end of each kick
Swim:	200 Breaststroke – find the high and low chest positions in each stroke
Drill:	100 Breaststroke With Dolphin – breathe above hip line
Drill:	100 Breaststroke With Dolphin – streamline below hip line
Swim:	200 Breaststroke – breathe up and streamline down in each stroke
Drill:	100 Shoot to Streamline – use hips to balance upper body actions
Drill:	100 Shoot to Streamline – use hips to balance kick
Swim:	200 Breaststroke – feel your hips as the balance point of the stroke
Swim:	4 x 25 Breaststroke w/10 SR – holding your balance point
Cool-down:	100
Total:	1,800 + 2 min. stationary drills

WORKOUT 53

FOCUS POINT:	Breaststroke foot position and ankle rotation
Warm-up:	200
Kick:	300 – other than breaststroke kick
Drill:	Flex/Point – 2 min.
Drill:	Duck Feet – 5 min.
Kick:	4 x 25 Breaststroke kick w/10 SR – focus on flexing feet
Kick:	4 x 25 Breaststroke kick w/10 SR – focus on holding on to water with sole of feet
Kick:	4 x 25 Breaststroke kick w/10 SR – focus on ankle rotation throughout kick
Drill:	Vertical Breaststroke Kick – 1 min. – focus on flexing feet
Drill:	Vertical Breaststroke Kick – 1 min. – focus on holding on to water with sole of feet
Drill:	Vertical Breaststroke Kick – 1 min. – focus on ankle rotation throughout kick
Swim:	4 x 50 Breaststroke w/15 SR – focus on flexing feet
Swim:	4 x 50 Breaststroke w/15 SR – focus on holding on to water with sole of feet
Swim:	4 x 50 Breaststroke w/15 SR – focus on ankle rotation throughout kick
Cool-down:	100
Total:	1,500 + 10 min. stationary drills

WORKOUT 54

FOCUS POINT:	Circle feet around knees
Warm-up:	200
Kick:	200 – other than breaststroke kick
Drill:	Vertical Breaststroke Kick – 1 min. – position knees shoulder-width apart
Drill:	Vertical Breaststroke Kick – 1 min. – knees closer together than feet
Swim:	4 x 50 Breaststroke w/15 SR – knees shoulder-width apart, closer together than feet
Drill:	50 Breaststroke Kick on Back – keep knees shoulder-width apart
Drill:	50 Breaststroke Kick on Back – keep feet outside knees
Swim:	4 x 50 Breaststroke w/15 SR – knees shoulder-width apart, feet outside knees
Drill:	50 Head-Up Breaststroke Kick – arms leading – knees stay shoulder-width apart
Drill:	50 Head-Up Breaststroke Kick – head leading – sweep wide to narrow with feet
Swim:	4 x 50 Breaststroke w/15 SR – knees shoulder-width apart, sweep wide to narrow with feet
Drill:	50 Head-Up Breaststroke Kick – arms leading – stable knees
Drill:	50 Head-Up Breaststroke Kick – head leading – circle feet around knees
Swim:	4 x 50 Breaststroke w/15 SR – stable knees, circle feet around knees
Swim:	4 x 25 Breaststroke w/10 SR – stable knees, shoulder-width apart, circle feet around knees
Cool-down:	100
Total:	1,700 + 2 min. stationary drills

WORKOUT 55

FOCUS POINT:	Minimize bend at hips
Warm-up:	200
Kick:	200 – other than breaststroke kick
Drill:	200 Breaststroke Kick on Back – draw heel up behind you
Drill:	200 Breaststroke Kick on Back with kickboard over knees – keep knees underwater
Swim:	4 x 50 Breaststroke w/15 SR – minimal bend at hips
Drill:	Vertical Breaststroke Kick – 1 min. – achieve straight line from shoulder to knee
Drill:	Vertical Breaststroke Kick – 1 min. – avoid bobbing bending at the hip
Swim:	4 x 50 Breaststroke w/15 SR – minimal bend at hips
Drill:	200 Head-Up Breaststroke Kick – head leading – feel heels with fingertips
Drill:	200 Head-Up Breaststroke Kick – head leading – avoid drag of folding at the hip
Swim:	4 x 50 Breaststroke w/15 SR – minimal bend at hips
Cool-down:	100
Total:	1,900 + 2 min. stationary drills

WORKOUT 56

FOCUS POINT:	Keep heels underwater
Warm-up:	200
Kick:	200 – other than breaststroke kick
Swim:	8 x 50 alternating 50s of Freestyle/Breaststroke w/15 SR
Drill:	4 x 25 Head-Up Breaststroke Kick w/10 SR – listen for absolutely quiet kick
Swim:	4 x 50 Breaststroke w/15 SR – kick should never break the surface
Drill:	4 x 25 3 Kick Breaststroke w/10 SR – avoid snagging air with feet
Swim:	4 x 50 Breaststroke w/15 SR – keep heels underwater
Drill:	Rocking Drill – 1 min. – rock chest up to increase water over raised heels
Swim:	200 Breaststroke – incorporate rocking motion to keep heels underwater
50 Easy	
Swim:	4 x 25 Fast Breaststroke – keep heels underwater by rocking
Cool-down:	100
Total:	1,850 + 1 min. stationary drills

WORKOUT 57

FOCUS POINT:	Accelerate your kick
Warm-up:	200
Kick:	8 x 50 – other than breaststroke kick
Drill:	Vertical Breaststroke Kick – 30 sec. – use slow kick
Drill:	Vertical Breaststroke Kick – 30 sec. – use fast kick – notice face stays above water better
Swim:	4 x 50 Breaststroke w/15 SR – use fast kick
Drill:	100 Head-Up Breaststroke Kick – arms leading – each kick finishes faster than it starts
Drill:	100 Head-Up Breaststroke Kick – head leading – each kick finishes faster than it starts
Swim:	4 x 50 Breaststroke w/15 SR – finish each kick fast
Drill:	100 3 Kick Breaststroke – accelerate your kick
Drill:	100 2 Kick Breaststroke – accelerate your kick
Swim:	4 x 50 Breaststroke w/15 SR – clap feet together at end of kick
Swim:	8 x 25 alternating 25s of Fast Breaststroke/Easy Breaststroke w/15 SR – accelerate your kick
Cool-down:	100
Total:	1,900 + 1 min. stationary drills

WORKOUT 58

FOCUS POINT:	Keep arm stroke small and forward
Warm-up:	200
Kick:	200 - other than breaststroke kick
Drill:	4 x 50 Sculling w/15 SR - hands stay forward
Swim:	200 Breaststroke - incorporate sculling motion
Drill:	4 x 50 Half Stroke Breaststroke w/15 SR - watch hands throughout stroke
Swim:	200 Breaststroke - keep hands within visual range
Drill:	4 x 50 Hand Speed Drill w/15 SR - small strokes make faster strokes
Swim:	200 Breaststroke - keep arm stroke small and forward
50 Easy	
Swim:	8 x 25 Breaststroke w/10 SR - watch hands, keep arm stroke small and forward
Cool-down:	100
Total:	1,950

WORKOUT **59**

FOCUS POINT:	No chicken wings!
Warm-up:	200
Kick:	200 – other than breaststroke kick
Drill:	4 x 50 Sculling w/15 SR – feel outsweep and insweep
Swim:	8 x 25 Breaststroke w/10 SR – keep elbows high until end of insweep
Drill:	4 x 25 Breaststroke With Fists w/10 SR – elbows follow hands inward at insweep
Drill/Swim:	200 – alternating 25s of Breaststroke With Fists/ Breaststroke – hands, then elbows
Drill:	8 x 25 Half Stroke Breaststroke w/10 SR – keep elbows in front of rib cage
Swim:	4 x 50 Breaststroke w/15 SR – keep elbows from slipping behind rib cage
Drill/Swim:	200 – alternating 25s of Hand Speed Drill/Breaststroke – fold elbows in front of rib cage
Swim:	8 x 25 Breaststroke w/10 SR – no chicken wings!
Cool-down:	100
Total:	2,000

WORKOUT 60

FOCUS POINT:	Hold on to the water through the corners
Warm-up:	200
Kick:	300 – other than breaststroke kick
Drill:	200 Sculling – hold on to water through outsweep and insweep
Swim:	8 x 50 Breaststroke w/15 SR – feel the corners
Drill:	8 x 50 Corners Drill w/15 SR – don't let go of the water
Swim:	200 Breaststroke – hold on to the water in both directions
Swim:	4 x 25 Breaststroke w/10 SR – feel the corners
Swim:	4 x 25 Breaststroke w/10 SR – hold on to the water through the corners
Cool-down:	100
Total:	2,000

WORKOUT 61

FOCUS POINT:	Getting through the drag point
Warm-up:	200
Kick:	300 – other than breaststroke kick
Swim:	200 Breaststroke w/15 SR – notice any halt in arm stroke at end of insweep
Drill:	8 x 25 Head-Up Breaststroke w/10 SR – identify the halt at the drag point
Drill:	4 x 50 Breaststroke With Fists w/15 SR – feel the halt at the drag point
Swim:	200 Breaststroke – feel the effect of the drag point
Drill:	4 x 50 Hand Speed Drill w/15 SR – eliminate halt at end of insweep
Swim:	200 Breaststroke – get through the drag point quickly
Drill:	100 Shoot to Streamline – get through the drag point
Swim:	4 x 25 alternating 25s of Fast Breaststroke/Easy Freestyle w/15 SR – eliminate the drag point
Cool-down:	100
Total:	2,000

WORKOUT 62

FOCUS POINT:	Get back to home base
Warm-up:	200
Kick:	300 – other than breaststroke kick
Swim:	8 x 25 Breaststroke w/10 SR – feel the home base starting point of each stroke
Swim:	8 x 25 Breaststroke w/10 SR – feel the home base ending point of each stroke
Drill:	200 Head-Up Breaststroke – watch hands touch home base after each stroke
Swim:	4 x 50 Breaststroke w/15 SR – start each new stroke from home base
Swim:	200 Breaststroke – strike home base between each stroke
Drill:	2 x 100 Shoot to Streamline w/15 SR – shoot to home base
Swim:	8 x 25 Breaststroke w/15 SR – get back to home base
Cool-down:	100
Total:	2,000

WORKOUT 63

FOCUS POINT:	Lean into your recovery
Warm-up:	200
Kick:	8 x 25 – other than breaststroke kick w/10 SR
Swim:	200 Breaststroke – focus on achieving a productive streamline
Drill:	4 x 25 Rocking Drill w/10 SR – shift weight forward approaching streamline
Swim:	200 Breaststroke – streamline downhill after recovery
Swim:	200 Breaststroke – streamline downhill, balance on your chest
Drill:	4 x 25 Grow Your Recovery w/10 SR – lean into your recovery
Swim:	200 Breaststroke – shift weight forward into recovery
Swim:	200 Breaststroke – use narrow recovery
Drill:	4 x 25 Shoot to Streamline w/10 SR – narrow, quick recovery
Swim:	200 Breaststroke – narrow, quick recovery to downhill streamline
Cool-down:	100
Total:	2,000

WORKOUT 64

FOCUS POINT:	Unified arm stroke and breathing action
Warm-up:	200
Kick:	200 – other than breaststroke kick
Drill:	4 x 50 Corners Drill w/10 SR – feel lift at the corners
Drill:	4 x 50 Corners Drill w/10 SR – feel face rise during insweep
Swim:	200 Breaststroke – inhale as face rises during insweep
Drill:	4 x 50 Fold and Shrug w/10 SR – feel weight shifting forward after inhale
Drill:	4 x 50 Fold and Shrug w/10 SR – feel face return to water between extended arms
Swim:	200 Breaststroke – exhale in streamline position
50 Easy	
Swim:	8 x 25 Fast Breaststroke w/15 SR – feel unified arm stroke and breathing action
Cool-down:	100
Total:	1,950

WORKOUT 65

FOCUS POINT:	Find the natural high point
Warm-up:	200
Kick:	200 – other than breaststroke kick
Drill:	Rocking Drill – 1 min. – feel the high point of the head
Drill:	Rocking Drill – 1 min. – feel the high point of the heels
Swim:	8 x 50 Breaststroke w/15 SR – feel the natural high point
Drill:	100 Shoot to Streamline – feel the high point of the head and heels
Drill:	100 Shoot to Streamline – inhale at the high point of head and heels
Swim:	7 x 50 Breaststroke w/15 SR – feel the natural high point
Drill:	100 Inhale at the High Point – inhale at the high point of head and heels
Drill:	100 Inhale at the High Point – inhale before recovery and kick
Swim:	6 x 50 Breaststroke w/15 SR – feel the natural high point before recovery and kick
Cool-down:	100
Total:	1,950

WORKOUT 66

FOCUS POINT:	Look at the water while inhaling
Warm-up:	200
Kick:	300 – other than breaststroke kick
Swim:	100 Breaststroke – count strokes
Swim:	100 Breaststroke – look forward, count strokes, compare
Swim:	100 Breaststroke – look down at the water, count strokes, compare
Drill:	4 x 50 Eyes on the Water w/15 SR – look down at the water
Drill:	4 x 50 Corners Drill w/15 SR – watch hands at corners
Drill:	4 x 50 Shoot to Streamline w/15 SR – watch hands transition to recovery
Drill:	4 x 50 Fold and Shrug w/15 SR – look at the water while inhaling
Swim:	100 Breaststroke – count strokes, compare
Swim:	8 x 25 Breaststroke w/10 SR – eyes on the water
Cool-down:	100
Total:	2,000

WORKOUT 67

FOCUS POINT:	No nodding!
Warm-up:	200
Kick:	8 x 50 w/10 SR – other than breaststroke kick
Swim:	200 Breaststroke – shift weight forward from chest
Swim:	100 Breaststroke – accelerate hands on insweep
Swim:	50 Breaststroke – inhale at the natural high point
Drill/Swim:	12 x 25 alternating 25s of Tennis Ball Drill/Breaststroke – don't drop ball while inhaling
Swim:	200 Breaststroke – look down at the water throughout stroke
Swim:	100 Breaststroke – use rocking motion from core
Swim:	50 Breaststroke – lean into recovery with chest
Drill/Swim:	12 x 25 alternating 25s of Tennis Ball Drill/Breaststroke – no nodding
Cool-down:	100
Total:	2,000

WORKOUT 68

FOCUS POINT:	Power from the core
Warm-up:	200
Kick:	12 x 25 alternating 25s of fast/easy w/10 SR – other than breaststroke kick
Drill:	100 Corners Drill – feel lift
Drill:	100 Breaststroke With Dolphin – exaggerate the lift
Drill/Swim:	100 alternating 25s of Breaststroke With Dolphin/ Breaststroke – achieve lift
Drill:	100 Rocking Drill – feel high and low chest positions
Drill:	100 Breaststroke With Dolphin – exaggerate high and low chest positions
Drill/Swim:	100 alternating 25s of Breaststroke With Dolphin/ Breaststroke – achieve high and low chest positions
Drill:	100 Fold and Shrug – feel weight shift forward
Drill:	100 Breaststroke With Dolphin – exaggerate weight shifting forward
Drill/Swim:	100 alternating 25s of Breaststroke With Dolphin/ Breaststroke – achieve forward shift of weight
Drill:	100 Shoot to Streamline – feel the downhill streamline
Drill:	100 Breaststroke With Dolphin – exaggerate the downhill streamline
Drill/Swim:	100 alternating 25s of Breaststroke With Dolphin/ Breaststroke – achieve the downhill streamline
Swim:	8 x 25 Breaststroke w/10 SR – achieve power from the core
Cool-down:	100
Total:	2,000

WORKOUT 69

FOCUS POINT:	Overcoming flat breaststroke
Warm-up:	200
Kick:	300 – other than breaststroke kick
Drill:	200 Breaststroke With Dolphin – feel rocking motion
Drill/Swim:	6 x 50 alternating Breaststroke With Dolphin/Breaststroke w/15 SR – feel rocking motion
Swim:	200 Breaststroke – feel rocking motion
Drill:	200 Breaststroke Alternating Dolphin and Breaststroke Kick – use rocking motion
Drill/Swim:	6 x 50 alternating Breaststroke Alternating Dolphin and Breaststroke Kick/Breaststroke w/15 SR – use rocking motion
Swim:	200 Breaststroke – use rocking motion
Cool-down:	100
Total:	2,000

WORKOUT 70

FOCUS POINT:	Breaststroke sequence
Warm-up:	200
Kick:	200 – other than breaststroke kick
Swim:	100 Breaststroke – focus on starting the arm stroke from streamline
Swim:	100 Breaststroke – focus on starting the inhale at the corners
Swim:	100 Breaststroke – focus on starting the kick when the arms are in mid recovery
Swim:	100 Breaststroke – focus on achieving complete streamline after the kick
Drill:	8 x 50 Stroke, Breathe, Kick, Glide Mantra
Swim:	8 x 50 Breaststroke w/10 SR – maintain the sequence of stroke elements
50 Easy	
Swim:	6 x 25 alternating 25s of Fast Breaststroke/Easy Breaststroke – maintain the sequence
Cool-down:	100
Total:	2,000

WORKOUT 71

FOCUS POINT:	Coordinated breaststroke
Warm-up:	200
Kick:	300 – other than breaststroke kick
Drill:	100 Corners Drill – find the high point in the stroke
Drill:	100 Inhale at the High Point – inhale the high point of the stroke
Swim:	8 x 50 Breaststroke w/15 SR – stroke up to breathe
Drill:	100 Breaststroke Alternating Dolphin and Breaststroke Kick – kick and achieve downhill streamline
Drill:	100 Shoot to Streamline – kick follows arms to streamline
Swim:	8 x 50 Breaststroke w/15 SR – kick down to streamline
Drill:	4 x 25 Stroke Up to Breathe, Kick Down to Glide w/10 SR – feel coordination
Swim:	4 x 25 Fast Breaststroke w/15 SR – stroke up to breathe, kick down to glide
Cool-down:	100
Total:	2,000

WORKOUT 72

FOCUS POINT:	Avoiding drag
Warm-up:	200
Kick:	200 – other than breaststroke kick
Drill:	8 x 25 Hand Speed Drill w/10 SR – no halt, get back to home base
Drill:	4 x 50 Half Stroke Breaststroke w/15 SR – keep stroke small, quick and forward
Swim:	100 Breaststroke – avoid drag in arm stroke from halting and over-size stroke
Drill:	8 x 25 Breaststroke Kick on Back w/10 SR – straight line from knees to shoulders
Drill:	4 x 50 Head-Up Breaststroke Kick w/15 SR – knees closer together than heels
Swim:	100 Breaststroke – avoid drag in kick from folded hips and unstable knee position
Drill:	8 x 25 Eyes on the Water w/10 SR – look down at the water
Drill:	4 x 50 Fold and Shrug w/15 SR – shift weight forward into streamline
Swim:	100 Breaststroke – avoid drag in breathing from looking forward and stopping momentum
Cool-down:	100
Total:	2,000

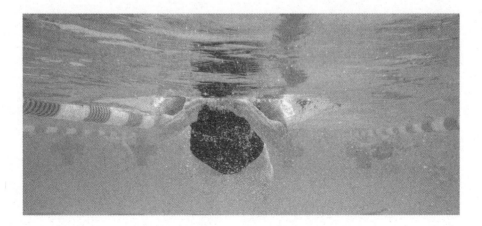

WORKOUT 73

FOCUS POINT:	Breaststroke tempo
Warm-up:	200
Kick:	8 x 25 w/10 SR – other than breaststroke kick
Drill:	4 x 50 No Stars – think arms, then legs
Swim:	200 Breaststroke – increase tempo, think arms, then legs
Swim:	100 Breaststroke – increase tempo, think arms, then legs
Swim:	50 Breaststroke – increase tempo, think arms, then legs
Swim:	25 Breaststroke – increase tempo, think arms, then legs
50 Easy	
Drill:	4 x 50 Glide Length, Glide Speed w/10 SR
Swim:	200 Breaststroke – think arms, then legs
Swim:	100 Breaststroke – increase tempo, maintain arms, then legs
Swim:	50 Breaststroke – increase tempo, maintain arms, then legs
Swim:	25 Breaststroke – increase tempo, maintain arms, then legs
50 Easy	
Swim:	8 x 25 alternating 25s of Fast Breaststroke/Freestyle w/15 SR – maintain arms, then legs
Cool-down:	100
Total:	1,950

WORKOUT 74

FOCUS POINT:	Maximizing power, minimizing drag
Warm-up:	200
Kick:	200 – other than breaststroke kick
Drill:	200 Breaststroke With Dolphin – feel rocking motion
Drill:	200 Breaststroke Alternating Dolphin and Breaststroke Kick – feel power from the core
Swim:	4 x 25 Breaststroke w/10 SR – achieve rocking motion and generate power from the core
Drill:	200 No Stars – arms, then legs
Drill:	200 Half Stroke Breaststroke – quick, forward arm stroke
Swim:	4 x 25 Breaststroke w/10 SR – achieve good timing to avoid drag
Drill:	200 Shoot to Streamline – get through the drag point back to home base
Drill:	200 Thread the Needle – aim your power forward
Swim:	4 x 25 Breaststroke w/10 SR – minimize drag and maximize power
Cool-down:	100
Total:	2,000

WORKOUT 75

FOCUS POINT:	Finding your stroke count
Warm-up:	200
Kick:	200 – other than breaststroke kick
Swim:	200 Freestyle – count strokes
Swim:	200 Breaststroke – count strokes (aim for half your freestyle count)
Swim:	200 alternating 25s of Freestyle/Breaststroke – count strokes
Drill:	4 x 50 Fist Freestyle w/15 SR
Drill:	4 x 50 Breaststroke With Fists w/15 SR
Swim:	200 Freestyle – count strokes
Swim:	200 Breaststroke – count strokes
Swim:	200 alternating 25s of Freestyle/Breaststroke – count strokes (aim for half your freestyle count)
Cool-down:	100
Total:	2,000

TECHNIQUE WORKOUTS FOR BUTTERFLY

WORKOUT 76

FOCUS POINT:	Butterfly body motion
Warm-up:	200
Kick:	300 your choice
Drill:	Bowing – 2 min.
Drill:	4 x 25 Weight Shifting – head leading w/15 SR – horizontal bowing
Drill:	4 x 25 Weight Shifting – head leading w/15 SR – hips remain high
Drill:	4 x 25 Weight Shifting – head leading w/15 SR – use abdominals to shift weight
Drill:	4 x 50 Body Wave – head leading w/15 SR – head to hips
Drill:	4 x 50 Body Wave – hands leading w/15 SR – hands to hips
Drill:	4 x 50 Body Wave – head leading w/15 SR – head to hips to feet
Drill:	4 x 50 Body Wave – hands leading w/15 SR – hands to hips to feet
Cool-down:	100
Total:	1,700 + 2 min. stationary drills

WORKOUT 77

FOCUS POINT:	Maintain high hips
Warm-up:	200
Kick:	200 your choice
Drill:	200 Dipping – maintain high hips
Drill:	200 Body Wave head leading – roll the wave through hips
Drill:	8 x 25 Deep to Shallow Dolphin w/10 SR – maintain high hips
Drill:	200 Dipping – low chest, high hips
Drill:	200 Body Wave hands leading – roll the wave through hips
Drill:	8 x 25 Deep to Shallow Dolphin w/10 SR – balance from hips
Cool-down:	100
Total:	1,700

WORKOUT 78

FOCUS POINT:	Kick action ends at the feet
Warm-up:	200
Kick:	300 your choice
Drill:	8 x 25 Dipping w/10 SR – chest begins action
Drill:	4 x 50 Body Wave head leading w/15 SR – roll the wave chest to hips
Drill:	200 Deep to Shallow Dolphin – roll the wave through the hips
Drill:	4 x 50 Body Wave head leading w/15 SR – roll the wave chest to hips to the feet
Drill:	8 x 25 Deep to Shallow Dolphin w/10 SR – feet follow the head
Drill:	200 Breaststroke With Dolphin – kick action ends at the feet
Cool-down:	100
Total:	1,800

WORKOUT 79

FOCUS POINT:	Fluid dolphin action
Warm-up:	200
Kick:	200 your choice
Drill:	8 x 25 Dipping w/10 SR – rhythmic dip
Drill:	8 x 50 Body Wave w/15 SR – rhythmic wave
Drill:	8 x 50 Deep to Shallow Dolphin w/15 SR – rhythmic wave
Drill:	Vertical Dolphin – 30 sec. – keep head above water
Drill:	Vertical Dolphin – 30 sec. – flip each kick down to the feet
Drill:	Vertical Dolphin – 30 sec. – rhythmic wave
Drill:	4 x 50 Deep to Shallow Dolphin w/15 SR – fluid, rhythmic wave
Kick:	4 x 25 Dolphin - hands leading w/10 SR – fluid dolphin action
Cool-down:	100
Total:	1,800 + 1.5 min. stationary drills

WORKOUT 80

FOCUS POINT:	Feeling full body dolphin
Warm-up:	200
Kick:	300 your choice
Drill:	4 x 25 Weight Shifting w/10 SR – use your abdominals
Drill:	8 x 25 Body Wave w/10 SR – roll the action down from chest to feet
Drill:	4 x 50 Dolphin Dives – feel your body and legs follow your head
Drill:	200 Breaststroke With Dolphin – body and legs follow your head
Drill:	4 x 50 Dolphin Dives – faster tempo
Drill:	8 x 25 Body Wave w/10 SR – feel full body dolphin
Cool-down:	100
Total:	1,900

WORKOUT 81

FOCUS POINT:	Kick water not air
Warm-up:	200
Kick:	300 your choice
Drill:	200 Body Wave – rhythmic action
Drill:	200 Body Wave with fins – low knee bend, keep feet connected to water
Drill:	200 Body Wave – low knee bend, keep feet connected to water
Drill:	200 Deep to Shallow Dolphin – rhythmic action
Drill:	200 Deep to Shallow Dolphin with fins – keep fins connected to water
Drill:	200 Deep to Shallow Dolphin – keep feet connected to water
Kick:	8 x 25 dolphin – hands leading w/10 SR – kick water not air
Cool-down:	100
Total:	2,000

WORKOUT 82

FOCUS POINT:	Snapping your kick downward
Warm-up:	200
Kick:	200 your choice
Drill:	200 Body Wave – whip-like action from chest to feet
Kick:	200 dolphin kick – hands leading – whiplike action from hands to feet
Drill:	Vertical Dolphin – 1 min. – snap forward, relax back
Drill:	4 x 25 Back Dolphin w/10 SR – snap up, relax down
Kick:	200 dolphin kick – snap down, relax up
Drill:	200 Body Wave – kick snaps down when chest is high
Kick:	200 dolphin kick – avoid raising heels and head at the same time
Drill:	Vertical Dolphin – 1 min. – snap forward, relax back
Drill:	4 x 25 Back Dolphin w/10 SR – snap up, relax down
Kick:	200 dolphin kick – snap down, relax up
Cool-down:	100
Total:	1,900 + 2 min. stationary drills

WORKOUT 83

FOCUS POINT:	Think double arm freestyle
Warm-up:	200
Kick:	8 x 50 your choice w/10 SR
Swim:	4 x 50 Freestyle w/15 SR – focus on the three-dimensional sweep of the arm stroke
Drill:	4 x 25 Tracing Question Marks – w/15 SR – trace wide to narrow question marks
Drill:	4 x 25 Tracing Question Marks – w/15 SR – trace deep to shallow question marks
Swim:	4 x 50 Freestyle w/15 SR – focus on reaching forward before starting stroke
Drill:	4 x 25 Tracing Question Marks – w/15 SR – reach forward before each stroke
Drill:	4 x 25 Tracing Question Marks – w/15 SR – reach forward into each stroke
Swim:	4 x 50 Freestyle w/15 SR – focus on the front to back direction of the arm stroke
Drill:	4 x 25 Tracing Question Marks – w/15 SR – avoid pressing down to start stroke
Drill:	4 x 25 Tracing Question Marks – w/15 SR – stroke from front to back
Cool-down:	100
Total:	1,900

WORKOUT 84

FOCUS POINT:	Pull, then push
Warm-up:	200
Kick:	300 alternating 50s of flutter kick/dolphin
Drill:	200 Pull/Push Freestyle – feel pull
Drill:	200 Pull/Push Freestyle – feel push
Drill:	4 x 25 One-Arm Fly w/15 SR – feel pull
Drill:	4 x 25 One-Arm Fly w/15 SR – feel push
Drill:	200 Pull/Push Freestyle – feel pull
Drill:	200 Pull/Push Freestyle – feel push
Drill:	4 x 25 Tracing Question Marks w/15 SR – feel pull
Drill:	4 x 25 Tracing Question Marks w/15 SR – feel push
Swim:	4 x 25 alternating 25s of Freestyle/Butterfly w/15 SR – feel pull, then push
Cool-down:	100
Total:	1,900

137

WORKOUT 85

FOCUS POINT:	Accelerate the arm stroke
Warm-up:	200
Kick:	200 alternating 25s of dolphin/flutter
Swim:	8 x 50 Freestyle – w/15 SR – feel arm stroke accelerate toward the back
Drill:	4 x 50 One-Arm Butterfly w/15 SR – accelerate stroke toward the back
Swim:	8 x 50 Freestyle – w/15 SR – feel stroke gain speed from front to back
Drill:	4 x 50 One-Arm Butterfly w/15 SR – stroke gains speed from front to back
Drill:	8 x 25 Left Arm, Right Arm, Both Arms w/15 SR – accelerate the arm stroke
Cool-down:	100
Total:	1,900

WORKOUT 86

FOCUS POINT:	Finish outward
Warm up:	200
Kick:	200 your choice
Swim:	8 x 50 Freestyle w/15 SR – press back to finish stroke
Drill:	4 x 25 Tracing Question Marks w/15 SR – press out to finish stroke
Drill:	200 One-Arm Butterfly – quick press out to finish stroke
Swim:	200 Freestyle – quick press back to finish stroke
Drill:	8 x 50 Left Arm, Right Arm, Both Arms w/15 SR – quick press out to finish stroke
Drill/Swim:	8 x 25 alternating 25s of Round-off"/Freestyle w/15 SR – quick finish, out on fly, back on free
Cool-down:	100
Total:	2,000

WORKOUT 87

FOCUS POINT:	Positive recovery
Warm up:	200
Kick:	8 x 25 dolphin alternating 25s of head leading/hands leading w/10 SR
Drill:	Recovery in Place – 30 sec. – thumbs up – notice negative recovery with elbows dragging through water
Drill:	Recovery in Place – 30 sec. – thumbs down – notice positive recovery with arms arching over the water
Drill/Swim:	8 x 25 – 6 strokes Pinkies Up then Freestyle w/ 15 SR – arms arch over the water
Drill/Swim:	8 x 25 – 6 strokes Pinkies Up, then Freestyle w/ 15 SR – thumbs down, pinkies up
Drill/Swim:	8 x 25 – 6 strokes Pinkies Up, then Freestyle w/ 15 SR – recovery clears the water
Drill:	8 x 50 One-Arm Butterfly w/15 SR – maintain pinkie up hand position throughout recovery
Drill:	4 x 50 Left Arm, Right Arm, Both Arms w/15 SR – positive recovery
Drill/Swim:	8 x 25 alternating 25s of Pinkies Up/Freestyle w/15 SR
Cool-down:	100
Total:	1,900 + 1 min. stationary drills

WORKOUT 88

FOCUS POINT:	Achieving a relaxed recovery
Warm-up:	200
Kick:	200 dolphin alternating 25s on front/on back
Swim:	8 x 50 Freestyle w/10 SR – emphasize a relaxed arm and hand throughout recovery
Drill:	8 x 25 One-Arm Butterfly w/15 SR – relax arm and hand throughout recovery
50 Easy	
Drill:	4 x 25 The Flop w/15 SR – generate recovery from chest
50 Easy	
Drill/Swim:	8 x 50 alternating 25s of One-Arm Butterfly/Freestyle – chest leads recovery, hands follow
50 Easy	
Drill:	4 x 25 The Flop w/15 SR – hand, wrist, arms and shoulders should be relaxed
50 Easy	
Swim:	4 x 25 alternating 25s of Butterfly/Freestyle w/15 SR – achieve a relaxed recovery
Cool-down:	100
Total:	2,000

WORKOUT 89

FOCUS POINT:	Enter wide and reach
Warm-up:	200
Kick:	200 your choice
Drill:	4 x 25 One-Arm Butterfly w/15 SR – hand enters out side of shoulder
Drill:	4 x 25 One-Arm Butterfly w/15 SR – push elbow to straight
Drill:	4 x 25 One-Arm Butterfly w/15 SR – reach forward with thumbs
Drill/Swim:	4 x 50 alternating 25s of Reaching to a "Y"/Freestyle w/15 SR – enter wide
Drill/Swim:	4 x 50 alternating 25s of Reaching to a "Y"/Freestyle w/15 SR – enter wider
Drill/Swim:	4 x 50 alternating 25s of Reaching to a "Y"/Freestyle w/15 SR – enter wide, push elbows to straight
Drill/Swim:	4 x 50 alternating 25s of Reaching to a "Y"/Freestyle w/15 SR – enter wider, push elbows to straight
Drill/Swim:	4 x 50 alternating 25s of Reaching to a "Y"/Freestyle w/15 SR – enter wide, push elbow to straight, reach forward with thumbs
Drill/Swim:	4 x 50 alternating 25s of Reaching to a "Y"/Freestyle w/15 SR – enter wider, push elbow to straight, reach forward with thumbs
Cool-down:	100
Total:	2,000

WORKOUT 90

FOCUS POINT:	Balance on your chest
Warm-up:	200
Kick:	200 your choice
Swim:	8 x 50 Freestyle w/15 SR – swim downhill
Drill:	8 x 25 Advanced One-Arm Fly w/15 SR – balance on chest when arm enters
Drill/Swim:	8 x 25 – 6 strokes Reaching a "Y", then Freestyle w/15 SR - chest low when you reach the "Y"
Drill/Swim:	8 x 25 6 strokes Chest Balance, then Freestyle w/15 SR – chest low, hips high when arms enter
Swim:	8 x 50 alternating 25s of Butterfly/Freestyle w/15 SR – downhill balance
Swim:	4 x 25 Butterfly w/30 SR – balance on chest when arms enter
Cool-down:	100
Total:	2,000

WORKOUT 91

FOCUS POINT:	Grab and go . . . Don't lose your momentum
Warm up:	200
Kick:	8 x 25 dolphin w/10 SR – fluid action
Swim:	100 Freestyle – emphasizing unified entry, reach and catch action
Swim/Drill:	200 alternating 25s of Freestyle/One-Arm Butterfly – enter, reach and catch
Swim/Drill:	200 alternating 25s of Freestyle/Advanced One-Arm Butterfly – enter, reach and catch
Swim:	100 Freestyle – emphasizing continuous entry, reach and catch action
Swim/Drill:	200 alternating 25s of Freestyle/One-Arm Butterfly – maintain momentum at entry
Swim/Drill:	200 alternating 25s of Freestyle/Advanced One-Arm Butterfly – maintain momentum at entry
Drill/Swim:	8 x 25 No Pause Butterfly for 6 strokes, then Freestyle w/15 SR – grab water and go
Swim:	8 x 25 alternating 25s of Butterfly/Freestyle w/15 SR – Grab and go . . . don't lose your momentum
Cool-down:	100
Total:	1,900

WORKOUT 92

FOCUS POINT:	Inhale at the natural high point of the stroke
Warm-up:	200
Kick:	200 dolphin
Swim:	200 Freestyle – focus on the rhythmic breathing
Drill:	Breathing Timing Drill – 30 sec. – face in water with arms forward, face out with arms back
Drill:	Breathing Timing Drill – 30 sec. – face rises as arms pull back
Drill:	Breathing Timing Drill – 30 sec. – face descends as arms recover
Swim:	8 x 25 for 8 strokes Butterfly, then Freestyle w/15 SR – face rises as arms pull back
Swim:	8 x 25 for 8 strokes Butterfly, then Freestyle w/15 SR – face descends as arms recover
Drill:	200 Flying Dolphin Dives – feel the natural high point of the stroke
Drill:	200 Flying Dolphin Dives – inhale at the natural high point of the stroke
Swim:	200 Freestyle – focus on the continual inhale/exhale action
Drill:	Breathing Timing Drill – 30 sec. – exhale while face is in water
Drill:	Breathing Timing Drill – 30 sec. – inhale when face rises
Drill:	Breathing Timing Drill – 30 sec. – don't hold your breath!
Drill/Swim:	8 x 25 No Pause Butterfly 8 strokes, then Freestyle w/15 SR – inhale at the high point
Swim:	4 x 25 Butterfly w/20 SR – find the natural high point of the stroke and inhale
Cool-down:	100
Total:	2,000 + 3 min. stationary drills

WORKOUT 93

FOCUS POINT:	Look down at the water when inhaling
Warm-up:	200
Kick:	8 x 50 your choice w/10 SR
Swim:	8 x 50 Freestyle w/15 SR – focus on low profile breathing
Swim:	8 x 50 Breaststroke w/15 SR – focus on looking at the water while inhaling
Drill/Swim:	8 x 25 Eyes on the Water Butterfly for 8 strokes, then Freestyle w/15 SR – look down at the water
Swim:	8 x 25 alternating 25s of Butterfly/Breaststroke w/15 SR – look down at the water while inhaling
Cool-down:	100
Total:	1,900

WORKOUT 94

FOCUS POINT:	Breathe forward, not up!
Warm-up:	200
Kick:	200 your choice
Swim:	200 Freestyle w/15 SR – feel reach, then catch
Swim:	200 Freestyle w/15 SR – feel pull, then push
Drill:	200 One-Arm Butterfly – feel reach, catch, pull, push
Drill/Swim:	4 x 25 Tracing Question Marks for 8 strokes, then Freestyle w/ 15 SR – feel reach, catch, pull, push
Drill/Swim:	4 x 25 Tracing Question Marks for 8 strokes, then Freestyle w/ 15 SR – feel the front to back motion of each stroke
Drill:	Pitch to Press – 1 min. – focus on pitching hands to press back, not down on the water
Swim:	8 x 50 alternating 25s of Tracing Question Marks/ Freestyle w/15 SR – breathe forward, not up
Drill:	8 x 25 No Pause Butterfly for 10 strokes, then Freestyle w/15 SR – breathe forward while pressing back
Cool-down:	100
Total:	1,900 + 1 min. stationary drills

WORKOUT 95

FOCUS POINT:	Get your head back down quickly into the line of the stroke
Warm-up:	200
Kick:	200 dolphin
Swim:	8 x 50 Freestyle w/15 SR – focus on rhythmic breathing
Swim:	8 x 25 for 8 strokes Butterfly, then Freestyle w/15 SR – face rises as arms pull back
Swim:	8 x 25 for 8 strokes Butterfly, then Freestyle w/15 SR – face descends as arms recover
Drill:	4 x 25 Positive Recovery w/15 SR – feel arch recovery over water
50 Easy	
Drill:	4 x 25 The Flop w/15 SR – head descends with chest
50 Easy	
Drill:	4 x 25 Hammer and Nail w/15 SR – forehead hits water first, not chin
50 Easy	
Drill:	4 x 25 Reaching to a "Y" w/15 SR – head returns to the water before hands
50 Easy	
Swim:	4 x 25 Butterfly for 10 strokes, then Freestyle w/15 SR – get head back down into the line of the stroke
Cool-down:	100
Total:	2,000

WORKOUT 96

FOCUS POINT:	Finding your best breathing pattern
Warm up:	200
Kick:	8 x 50 your choice w/10 SR
Swim:	100 Freestyle – breathing every 2 strokes
Swim:	100 Freestyle – breathing every 3 strokes
Swim:	100 Freestyle – breathing every 4 strokes
Swim:	100 Freestyle – breathing every 5 strokes
Swim:	50 Butterfly w/15 SR – breathing every 4 strokes
Swim:	50 Butterfly w/15 SR – breathing every 3 strokes
Swim:	50 Butterfly w/15 SR – breathing every 2 strokes
Swim:	50 Butterfly w/15 SR – breathing every stroke
50 Easy	
Swim:	200 Freestyle with your most comfortable breathing pattern
Swim:	25 Butterfly – choose the breathing pattern that is most sustainable
Swim:	25 Butterfly – choose the breathing pattern that is most rhythmic
Swim:	25 Butterfly – choose the breathing pattern that is most fluid
Swim:	25 Butterfly – choose the breathing pattern that most comfortable
50 Easy	
Swim:	8 x 25 alternating 25s of Butterfly/Freestyle – find your best breathing pattern
Cool-down:	100
Total:	1,900

WORKOUT 97

FOCUS POINT:	Fitting two dolphins into each stroke
Warm-up:	200
Kick:	300 your choice
Drill:	100 Body Wave – feel the dolphin action start high in the body and snap down to the feet
Drill:	200 One-Arm Butterfly – feet snap down as arm enters and catches
Drill:	200 One-Arm Butterfly – feet snap down again as arm finishes underwater stroke
Swim:	4 x 25 Butterfly w/15 SR – kick and pull, kick and push
Drill/Swim:	4 x 25 No Kick Butterfly for 10 strokes, then Freestyle w/15 SR – incorporate the body wave
Drill/Swim:	4 x 25 No Kick Butterfly for 10 strokes, then Freestyle w/15 SR – avoid over-bending knees
Drill/Swim:	4 x 25 No Kick Butterfly for 10 strokes, then Freestyle w/15 SR – feel the dolphin roll down to your feet anyway
Drill:	100 Left Arm, Right Arm, Both Arms – two dolphins per stroke
Swim:	4 x 25 Butterfly w/15 SR - kick and pull, kick and push
50 Easy	
Swim:	4 x 25 Butterfly w/15 SR – kick to enter, kick to exit
Cool-down:	100
Total:	1,850

WORKOUT 98

FOCUS POINT:	Coordination: kick and catch
Warm-up:	200
Kick:	8 x 50 your choice w/15 SR
Drill:	8 x 50 Freestyle With Dolphin w/15 SR – hand strikes the water as feet snap down
Drill:	200 One-Arm Butterfly – feel kick and catch at the same time
Swim:	4 x 25 Butterfly w/15 SR – kick and catch
50 Easy	
Drill:	200 One-Arm Butterfly – feel kick and catch at the same time
Swim:	4 x 25 Butterfly w/15 SR – kick and catch
50 Easy	
Swim:	8 x 25 alternating 25s of Butterfly/Freestyle w/15 SR – feel shift of weight down and forward as you kick and catch
Cool-down:	100
Total:	2,000

WORKOUT 99

FOCUS POINT:	Coordination: Kick and finish
Warm-up:	200
Kick:	8 x 50 your choice w/15 SR
Drill:	8 x 50 Freestyle With Dolphin w/15 SR – hand quickly finishes stroke as feet snap down
Drill:	200 Advanced One-Arm Butterfly – feel kick and finish at the same time
Swim:	4 x 25 Butterfly w/15 SR – kick and finish
50 Easy	
Drill:	200 Advanced One-Arm Butterfly – feel kick and finish at the same time
Swim:	4 x 25 Butterfly w/15 SR – kick and finish
50 Easy	
Swim:	8 x 25 alternating 25s of Butterfly/Freestyle w/15 SR – feel forward lift as you kick and finish
Cool-down:	100
Total:	2,000

WORKOUT **100**

FOCUS POINT:	Butterfly coordination
Warm-up:	200
Kick:	8 x 50 alternating 50s of dolphin/flutter w/10 SR
Drill:	4 x 50 One-Arm Butterfly w/15 SR – rhythmic stroke, rhythmic dolphin
Drill:	4 x 50 Advanced One-Arm Butterfly w/15 SR – quick finish and kick at the same time
Drill:	4 x 25 Eyes on the Water Butterfly w/15 SR – breathe forward, not up
Swim:	4 x 25 Butterfly w/15 SR – emphasize fast round out finish of stroke
50 Easy	
Swim:	4 x 25 Butterfly w/15 SR – emphasize fast finish and simultaneous kick
50 Easy	
Swim:	4 x 25 Butterfly w/15 SR – emphasize fast finish, kick and inhale at the same time
50 Easy	
Drill/Swim:	200 alternating 25s of Coordination Checkpoint/Freestyle
50 Easy	
Swim:	4 x 25 Butterfly w/15 SR – notice yourself move forward while you finish fast, kick and inhale
Cool-down:	100
Total:	2,000

CONCLUSION

Congratulations on taking on the journey of improving your swimming efficiency by working on the technique of swimming. If you have made it through all or most of these workouts, you have traveled a long way on that journey. You have practiced positive body position, productive kicking, the path of the stroke, recovery, alignment, leverage and coordination. You are now equipped with an awareness of many important elements that affect swimming efficiency.

You might be asking where this journey ends. The fact is, it doesn't. Even the most accomplished swimmer continues to refine technique, forever reaching for even more efficient swimming. It is a lifelong quest. It is a continuing journey of discovery, worth every stroke.

CREDITS

Cover and interior design: Anja Elsen
Layout: Anja Elsen
Managing editor: Elizabeth Evans
Cover photo: © AdobeStock
Photography: Vince Corbella, Kurt Krueger, Avital Brodin, Nick Umemoto, Lynn Sun, Blythe Lucero
Interior illustrations: Blythe Lucero

Swimmers Appearing in the Photos:
Meredith Anderson, Vicky Augustine, Jennifer Barra, Pam Bennett, Cornelia Bleul-Gohlke, Jonas Brodin, Monique Comacchio, Kathryn Cohn, Sara Ebadi, Chris Fish, Kathryn Fletcher, Seth Goddard, Liam Goddfrey, Laura Howard, Caroline Howard, Rachel Howard, Ellen Johns, Eric Johnson, Tami Kasamatsu, Siobhan Langlois, Bonnie Lucero, Blythe Lucero, Elise Lusk, Jessica Moll, Mary Moorhead, Alvaro Pastor, Dave Robert, Lissa Suden, Ian Umemoto, Nick Umemoto.

Thanks to all the Berkeley swimming community for making the most of our water.

Thanks to Martinez, Demo, Lucky, Scott, Bob, Tailio, Fat Cat and Arrow's Sister & company for their support.